Mercifully Short Stories

Bill Schultz

First Published in 2017 by Level Heading

Copyright © Bernard Schultz

All rights reserved. Without limiting the rights under copyright reserved above, no part of this publication may be reproduced, stored in or introduced into a retrieval system, or transmitted, in any form or by any means (electronic, mechanical, photocopying, recording or otherwise), without the prior written permission of both the copyright owner and Level Heading.

ISBN: 978-0-6481726-1-1

A catalogue record for this book is available from the National Library of Australia

Text design and layout by Level Heading – levelheading.com
Edited by Bernard Schultz

Level Heading

Dedicated to:

The Schultz family of Port Broughton, Monteith and Reservoir.

Contents

Introduction	7
The Wild Irishman	13
Remember Old George	23
A Matter of Priority	28
Mad	36
Poor Chris	42
The End	50
The Spirit of the Snowies	56
Just Kate	65
Good Money	79
Let's Have a Beer	89
Mulvaney, of Course	96
Weekend	104
The Rock	113
Dark	123
The Vision Splendid	129
North to Paradise	137
Return to the North	151
That's the Spirit	160
Our Sergeant Major	170
Gone Bush	181
Winding Back	191

Introduction

THIS COLLECTION IS A tribute to my father who wrote these stories back in the early and mid-1970s and into the 1980s. During his lunchtimes, or if the weather made it impossible to work at being a drainer, Dad would sit in the car and write. Some of the stories are semi-autobiographical, these are set in Masons Flat (an alias for Monteith, South Australia), or feature Kunz & Hanrahan, Drainage Contractors.

Dad was born in 1922, in Port Broughton, north-west of Adelaide, on the eastern side of Spencer Gulf. Dad's father had gone there in the late 1800s and grew wheat on a pretty big farm at Ward's Hill, not far from Port Broughton. A couple of the stories let you know that, even though Dad was only six or so when they left the wheat farm, it was a very important part of his make-up. As evidence of this, read the very last story, Winding Back.

A little Methodist Church was built on the corner of the property at Ward's Hill, and this is where Dad's older sisters, all twelve of them! attended school. The church building was still standing in

1976 when Dad showed it to me on a trip there (see the pictures, next page).

The family left Port Broughton in about 1928 and moved to a dairy farm at Monteith, which is on a sweeping bend in the Murray River, about 10 kilometres from Murray Bridge. Dad grew up here. This is where he experienced school, which he didn't like, and dairying, also which he didn't like. His attitude to cows is made very clear in The Vision Splendid, his homage to Banjo Patterson.

The hall mentioned in the story Mad is still standing (see picture opposite), though it's looking very sorry for itself. The Roll of Honour in the hall was made by Dad, after WWII.

During the War, Dad was posted to Darwin. He didn't care much for the tropics (see the stories North to Paradise and Return to the North).

Dad left Monteith in 1950, with Anne Patricia, always known as Pat, Joan and me (aged a few months). Though he left South Australia, it was always, fondly, part of him.

Not all the stories are 'true to life'. Some of them are pure imagination. There's even a couple of ghost stories, for crying out loud! (See, The Spirit of the Snowies and That's the Spirit.)

Dad handed me the stories in the mid-1990s and said, 'Do with these what you like.' He even wrote a note, which I've got tucked away somewhere, handing copyright to me.

So, I digitised them all, which at that time meant retyping them all, and then editing them. I have tried, as much as possible to leave the words as original as possible. There are some minor alterations, where wordings have fallen out of use, or their usage has changed. The one thing that Dad was set on was the title for the collection.

I have loved editing Dad's stories. I'm sorry that I haven't got around to publishing them until now. Editing was an emotional experience, because quite a few times I could hear Dad's voice reading the words. There were turns of phrase and remembered quotes that made him seem very close. Dad's been gone nearly ten years, and still, hardly a day goes by when I don't think of him, and miss him.

I have my favourite stories in this collection – Mulvaney of Course, what a great title, it tells the story of a witch too beautiful to be a witch, and Winding Back, which shows how Dad remembered his early life in Port Broughton, but more than that it shows how much he valued his best friend.

New Methodist Church at Ward's Hill
The picture represents the contractor (Mr. Brerton) handing the key over to Mr. Goodridge (secretary of the Building Committee). From: Kapunda Herald, Fri 2 Sep 1904 Page 3. Found through trove.com.au

... and (right) as it was when I photographed it in about 1976.

The Institute Hall at Monteith, built in 1922. Photo taken in 2016.

Masons Flat

The Wild Irishman

WHAT'S IN A NAME? Well you might ask. If you were to hear someone mention a name such as Hans Herman Schwartz, you would immediately conjure up the image of solidity, strength and quiet capability that typified the average Australian citizen of Germanic descent who has been responsible for the opening up of much of rural Australia, especially South Australia.

When we came to live at Masons Flat on the lower Murray River, our next door neighbours were the Schwartz family, and they soon became our best friends. Big Herman, the strongest man I ever met, also the kindest, gentlest and happiest, was married to Bridget Ryan, who had, in fullness of time, brought four sons and five daughters into the world. The second son was Hans Herman.

In his battered, greasy cow-cockie's hat, muddy gumboots, solid cotton shirt and wrinkled dungarees, Hans carried himself with the swashbuckling, devil-may-care air of a buccaneer, in the true tradition of fiction's favourite freebooters. He was lean and dark; his almost black curls flashed shades of copper in the sunlight, and you could sense the surplus of energy in his quick movements and his lightness of step.

He could break a horse, or the heart of a fair maid, and never lost an opportunity to do either. There was never a dull moment when Hans was around. Even the cows loved him, I believe.

He never stayed at Masons for very long, and was never at any other place for long either. From the time he was seventeen he had travelled the length, the width and the depth of Australia by horse, train, bicycle, car, truck, wagon or on foot.

In his travels he'd tried his hand at most honest jobs, and quite a few that were – if you cared to believe his tall, wonderful and imaginative stories that he could tell for hours on end– somewhat shady.

Herman and Bridey never received letters from him. He'd never have time to write, but he was likely to walk in any time of day or night and whether he'd been away for a week or a year, would immediately pitch in with whatever work was being done at that particular time of the year, and there is always work to be done on a dairy farm. Maybe he'd stay a couple of days or weeks or even months, but while he was there he'd earn his keep, and when gone again, the home would seem quiet in comparison.

The only time I ever knew the Schwartz home to be quiet was on the odd occasion when I'd walk in of an evening and they would be kneeling around the big table in the large room they used as a kitchen, dining room, lounge room, living room and rumpus room that Herman had built right across the back of the house.

This custom of theirs of saying the Rosary every evening, no matter what, seemed strange to me, but to them it was as much a part of their day as breakfast, dinner and tea, and if any of the neighbours happened to come in at the time, Herman would say in his deep voice, 'Com' in and sit, ve von't be long,' and any further greeting would wait until their prayers were finished.

At all other times the big room was a lively, happy place where any of the people of Masons were made welcome, and if Hans was home from his wanderings, the merriment was doubled. He'd coax Bridey away from her mending or knitting to the piano, and his clear tenor voice would fill the room. Herman's booming bass, singing old Irish ballads in a thick German accent would break up the singing with laughter, so Hans would make up for it by singing some of Herman's favourites in faultless German, which, no doubt at all, is a language to be sung. The big back room was a place of music, laughter and fun.

Kate Schwartz was my age, and she and I almost always did our homework together at one end of the the big table. 'You'd never get it done without me to help you, Fergie,' she would often say. We were thus occupied one cold, windy, rainy night when the door opened and a quiet voice said, 'God save all here.'

Kate's chair crashed back and she flew across the room.

'It's Hans, Hans, Hans,' and she was in his arms, her feet a foot off the floor and her own arms were around his neck. Bridey, Herman and I were the only ones who hadn't moved.

Herman put down *The Advertiser* and smiled across at Bridey who returned the smile, as much as to say, 'We're all here.'

As they stood up, Hans was between them, his arms lightly across both their shoulders saying, 'But it's good to be home.' For a moment he was serious. Then his father received a resounding whack, where father should slap son, and Hans and Bridey were doing a jig around the room. No one else was serious again that night. Kate and I had to finish our homework just before school next morning.

As the dancing couple paused beside me, Hans said in mock surprise, 'Which of my brothers is this, and why hasn't he greeted me?' and he grabbed me by the arms, and lifting me clear off the floor said, 'Why, its young Ian Ferguson, and as tall as I am,' which was true until he put me down again.

'Oh, what a family I've got,' he said. 'I come in, wet to the skin and starving, and no one to say "Come and warm yourself at our fire while we feed you and find some dry clothes." Three miles I've walked from the siding in the cold and wet, a poor, out of work miner, and not even a dry shirt.' And he turned to Bridey, 'Perhaps, ma'm, your husband could spare me half of one of his shirts, but first, find a crust of bread or it's a shroud I'll be needin'.'

The meal that he packed away gave truth to the claim that he was starving, but he could still talk between mouthfuls.

'What have I been doing, you ask. I've been a mile below the ground digging coal in New South Wales. Now there's a job for real men. Every minute, you wait for the roof to come in on you, with a million tons of mountain pushing down on it while you gouge out the coal that's been waiting ten million years just for you to get your drill into it. There's good men in the mines, Kate darlin'. Better than you'll ever find for yourself on a dairy farm. There's no skinny Fergusons, who only want to play the fiddle, down the mines, girl. Bring your fiddle over tomorrow night, Fergie. There's no one down a mine can play it like a skinny Ferguson.'

Old Carl had been teaching me for over a year now and he was a fine teacher. I told Hans I would.

'See that you do,' and he turned to his older brother Brian. 'Will you never make an uncle of me? Sure, I can't do that for myself. And how's your team playing this year? If you need a good, fast centre-man who's never played for anyone except for Masons Flat Football Club, though every club in the state is after me, then I'm your man. If I kick the ball straight down your throat a dozen times every quarter, even you might be able to get a goal.'

Brian, the best full-forward in the Murray-Mallee, said they'd lost a few games, but he was sure they'd play in the finals and had a good show of taking out the Premiership.

'Then it looks as though your champion will be at home for – how long? – about six weeks? Don't count on me for the cricket season, though. The Poms will be out here, and I'm sure to be picked for our test team.'

If he'd ever bowled anyone out, or stayed at the wicket long enough to hit more than two or three wild boundaries, it would have been his best season. He was too impatient to field. Cricket just wasn't his game – too many quiet spots.

'Sure, if mining is so good, why did you leave?' asked Bridey.

'Well, because you were not down the mine with me, light of my life,' in exact imitation of her brogue.

'There were other reasons too, but that's a long story and you know I can't start a long story if I don't have a smoke, but how can a poor miner on the run from the cops buy himself a cigarette?' Which was as good a way as any of asking Brian for the makings. Having rolled and lit his cigarette, he leaned forward on his folded arms, and yet another of his long stories began.

'When I left here – Christmas time, wasn't it? – I went down to Adelaide and saw an ad in the paper for an accountant on a station in western New South Wales. Sure, I know I'm not an accountant, Mother dear, but I didn't tell them that, and you must admit that I look intelligent, and I can put two and two together. Besides, the fares were paid – one way – and the trip up gave me an opportunity to study a book on 'Station Management and Bookkeeping', and it's not my fault if the author wasn't an accountant either. By the time I'd got to Woolma Station I knew everything there was to know about sheep stations – anyway, I was a shearers' cook last year; I've still got the rope burns on my neck to prove it.'

'What about references?' someone butted in.

'Will you stop interrupting. Anyone can write references. I met this bloke in the Red Lion – well, you wouldn't want me dying of thirst, and look at the example my own father set me.' Herman's rumble of a laugh gave lie to the statement. 'And in half an hour he knew me well enough to give me a reference that would have got me into the diplomatic corps.

'Well, I had quite a pleasant trip up, and the manager was there to meet me at the railway Station in a Model-T that was sired by a kangaroo. I've had better rides on buck-jumpers than the forty miles in that – eighty miles, if you count the up and down as well as the along. When I got to the station, the boss, Len Young, took me to my quarters and said, "Come over to the house and have some lunch and meet my daughter." Len was a long, skinny, ugly character, worse than Fergie's old man – how's your dad and mum, Ian? Alec getting his share of the girls since I left? – so I didn't give his daughter much of a chance on winning any beauty contests. Anyway, we went to the house and into the kitchen. Len said, "This is my daughter Anne. Mr Schwartz is the new accountant."

'She was beautiful. Of course, after a long trip and hours and hours since I'd seen any girl, I'd have even given ugly Bertha a second look, but as soon as I saw Anne I knew, somehow or other, I'd have to learn how to keep station books.

'Nothing awful about that, Mum, I'm only human. The moment I saw Anne Young I knew that this was a job I had to hold, no matter what. She was tall, slim, and her hair was like Claire's ...' glancing up at his sister, '... only it was clean and shiny, and didn't look like a sheaf of hay that had come undone. All right, little sister, her hair was like yours. Maybe she even looked a bit like you, if you had a figure and a face. Anne was beautiful, and her eyes were big and grey and serious, and she looked straight into mine. I wished I could look at people as honestly and openly as she looked at me. Naturally, she liked the look of me, after all I've got all the good looks in the family. She was so beautiful that I just stood there, feeling weak in the knees, and shy, and didn't know what to say.

'She said she was pleased to meet me, and hoped I'd had a good trip up, and would like my job at Woolma, and if there was anything I wanted to just ask. I managed to stammer out some reasonably adequate answers, and wanted to tell her that everything in the world I could ever want was right there in the kitchen at Woolma.

'Of course I mean it, Mum – I always do.

'After the meal, I sat there dreaming of what life would be like if I owned Woolma Station and everything on it. Len and I had a smoke, and he supposed I'd like to see the office and go over the books. The office was sort of an afterthought that had been hung on the corner of the house, under the wide veranda, and it would have been a very unhappy cat that anyone tried to swing in it. It held a desk and a chair. One wall was all wide shelves that held a frightening collection of ledgers, account books and many years' supply of invoices, dockets and various other papers that worry the life out of station book-keepers. The only good thing about the whole set up was that its door and window looked along the verandah towards the kitchen, and if anyone came out, they could be seen from the office, and Anne was worth looking at.

'Len must have detected a look of dismay on my face. He grinned and said, "a big station needs a lot of looking after, but let the books wait till morning, and relax for the afternoon."

'When I wondered out loud if there was a saddle horse available, he said there were no quiet ponies, but if I thought I could handle Anne's grey, he was sure Anne wouldn't mind. I thought he had a cheek suggesting that the best rodeo rider in Australia might fall off a fat little pony he had quietened for his little girl, so I said I might manage to hang on.

'The fat little pony was sixteen hands and looked ready to win the Great Eastern. It was the next most beautiful thing on the station. Since it was already saddled, I figured that Anne was intending to ride off somewhere, and I thought that maybe she might need some protection.

'I said to Len that I didn't think I should take Anne's horse. I asked if there was anything else available. My nimble mind was telling me I should try to overcome my natural shyness with girls so I could offer myself as her protector. Len got the idea that I thought the grey looked too big to fall from, so he reckoned he'd stop me altogether, "There are half a dozen saddle horses in the yard. If you think you can catch one and put a saddle on it, help yourself, but I'd better get some work done." I thanked him and went off to the horseyard.

'The inmates were fairly ordinary, run-of-the-mill, station horses, so I picked out the one most likely to keep up with the grey if it happened to bolt with Anne, and I didn't have much trouble catching and saddling it.

'Anne came out as I mounted, no doubt to help me up if I fell off, so I raked my heel down my mount's nearside, so she couldn't see me do it. For a moment I thought I'd overdone it. I'm not a show-off! When I was satisfied that Anne knew I could ride, I cantered to where she now sat on the grey.

'She smiled and I nearly did fall off. She said, "I'm just going for a ride down to the creek. Silver needs the exercise, and I like a ride every afternoon when it's not too hot. Would you like to come?" She knew I would. "Dad was worried when you saddled Brown Bob, but I think you can manage him." I was right in thinking that Len might have been watching.

'Brown Bob and Silver were as sedate as you please, except that Bob developed the embarrassing habit of edging over a bit too close to the grey. Did I tell you Anne was beautiful?

'We rode along the creek for a couple of miles. The creek was really a string of elongated waterholes lined on both sides with gums and casuarinas. Anne talked about everything and nothing in particular, as though we were old friends. Then, after a brief trot back to the station – she rode as well as any horseman, but looked much better – she accepted my offer to unsaddle Silver and give him a rub down.

'By this time I was feeling like a real heel. She was so honest and trusting, and I was there under false pretences. But I was also determined to fight before I fled. So, next morning I was in the office at daybreak and, apart from meals, never left until midnight.

'In eighteen hours, I'd learned more about sheep stations than that bloke who wrote the book had ever known. After breakfast the next morning, I asked Len if he would come to the office for a few minutes, and when he did I told him I'd never kept books; except for the football club and the hall committee when I was sixteen. He was mad at first, and I thought I'd be walking forty miles to catch the next train. Then he quietened down and said, "Well, now what?" I told him how I'd gone through the books, which were kept in pretty good order, in spite of the first impression of chaos, and that I reckoned I could handle them. He said, "Try it for a couple of weeks – if you can't handle it, you'll be back at the railhead with no ticket and no pay."'

Hans paused, as though the story was over. There was a flurry of questions.

'How long was I there? I left last week. What coal mine? Mum, you know what a liar I've always been. Oh yes, some of the story is true, but you'll have to work out how much.'

'What do you mean, "What about the girl?" Well she and her father are staying at Mrs Greg's guesthouse in town for a few days. I had tea with them tonight, before I got the train to the siding. Len has some business in Adelaide, he's buying Woolma Station – if he and I can raise enough money – then I'm going to marry Anne and keep his books for him.'

Masons Flat won the flag that year, without the champion centre-man.

Remember Old George

GEORGE BARKER WAS A long, lean, lugubrious beanpole of a man, and something of a professional pessimist. That was the only thing he ever took on that never showed a sound profit, so maybe he was only an amateur after all. A thorough type in everything he did, but what a grizzle guts. Dad used to say, 'He's also a thorough bastard'.

We knew him for years, and no matter what he did, he whined about the ultimate result. 'Sold half-a-dozen head on Tuesday because prices have been good. Twelve quid a piece – would've got thirteen last week. Just my luck.' Then he'd look as if he was fighting to keep back tears, and never thought to mention the fact that another seventy-odd pounds had joined the original half crown he'd got for the first rabbit skins he'd ever sold. Less commission, of course. 'They get it for doin' nothin'.' Mr Barker wasn't a big spender, unless he was sure of making a whacking big profit on what he spent.

He knew how to run a farm though. His cows were never too thin or too fat, always came in when the pastures were at their best, and there were more milk cans on his stand than on anyone else's along the road. 'Should be fillin' at least two more this time of the year, would be too if the spring rains'd kept up. Can't win in this game.' It was a bumper year, and even Dad had money in the bank.

Barker was a confirmed bachelor. 'Should've got married years ago.' So the whole neighbourhood was rocked on its heels when he up and married the school teacher.

All us boys were crazy about Miss Johnson. She was little, and dark, pretty as a picture, and as lively as a cricket. You should have seen her throw a cricket ball. Mum said she should have been a boy. We didn't think so. I used to wish I was twice my age. She just never could have been a boy, and I thought it was a pretty silly thing for Mum to have said. She wasn't given to saying silly things either. Why, Miss Johnson was … but that's not the story. She has been Mrs George Barker for so long now that it doesn't matter.

In the fullness of time, George became the father of three sons, his only bit of really bad luck up until then. The dam came later of course. I'm not saying that it was bad luck to have three sons, especially on a dairy farm, it's just that they all looked like him.

Dad came in one night after talking to Mr Barker. 'The old coot says he should have never got married. Cripes, he's got the best farm, the fattest bank account and the prettiest wife, er, ah, bar one, in the district, and my shoulder is wet with his blasted tears because he can't save a penny anymore.'

When the Lawson farm was sold, Barker bought it for a song. The depression had hit by then, and he was the only one around with any money. He reckoned it would do for George Junior later on, so he put a share farmer on it in the meantime. The share farmer more or less survived, and George's take went into the bank. George reckoned that he shouldn't have thrown his bit of savings away on a farm, and sold it as soon as things began to pick up again. 'Sold the place too soon, would've made another five percent on it if I'd waited to the end of the year. Just my luck.' He had barely doubled his money, and the bank manager nearly kissed him, maybe he did.

By this time his dairy herd was nothing short of magnificent, and by seeing the right people and saying the right thing at the right time, he somehow got in through the back door of the inaccessible Stud Book. So he now ran the Glen Barker Stud, winning blue ribbons by the bagful, first at the local shows and then the Royal Adelaide. 'If I'd done it years ago I might be worth something now.' Poor old George's timing was never perfect.

The three boys were now getting old enough to do most of the work around the farm. Mrs Barker was still just as pretty, and popular, and she must have loved George. You just don't think of George and romance at the same time, but I guess he must have loved her too. There was no doubt that she was happy with her lot. 'Women run your life once they get their hooks into you, you'd've thought I'd had more sense than to get married at that age.' No one ever heard Mrs Barker complain, but now, when George sang his songs of grief, he had a backing of three for the chorus and their mother's eyes would sparkle as she said, 'You're as bad as your father.' She must have thought that they were just wonderful because she always bubbled with that funny little chuckle as she said it.

Dad and old George were leaning on the fence talking, and I was down the hill a few yards from them. That was the day we had a beaut thunderstorm. I looked across at Dad, he saw me and took his handkerchief out of his pocket. I turned away so George wouldn't see me laughing. It was Dad's way of saying, 'Old George is crying again.'

I finished replacing the broken fence post and left. Not long after that it started raining. Barker and Dad took shelter under a big old red gum, and for a few minutes visibility was zero as the rain bucketed down in an absolute flood. George said, 'Look at that stream of water coming down the edge of the road and going to waste. A bloke should've sunk a dam there years ago. Nothing grows in that corner anyway.'

Two days later he hired a dam sinker and soon had a good deep hole to catch the runoff from the road.

We never had much rain for a while and George could have irrigated his farm with his tears. 'I must've been a darn fool to waste my money like that on a dam with no water in it, no wonder I can't ever put anything by. They charged me a small fortune for digging it, and then tried to rob me for a full day when they finished at half past three the last day.'

Rain always came, eventually. After a good winter and an abnormally wet week to finish off spring, the new dam was overflowing, and Dad said, 'If that old goat ever dug a pick into the ground it'd come up with a gold nugget stuck to it, and he'd whine because the digging was too hard.'

George said, 'I should've dug it bigger, but the price of windmills would break a man. I've had to fence it or I'd lose a beast in it for sure.' No, George couldn't do anything right, and I bet, wherever he is now, he's crying about all that money he couldn't take with him, and even if he could have, there isn't any way to invest it there. He drowned in the dam, you know.

It happened only a week after it filled. I was admiring the dam and wishing it was on our property when I sort of realised that he was floating face down in it. It was a weird feeling. I seemed to see him slowly and realise it suddenly. The raw, red earthworks were as slippery as soap, and after that first panicky shocking feeling of not knowing what to do, and all the thoughts that raced through my mind, like, poor Mrs Barker, who's to tell her? I went to the water's edge and went in after him, just in case he might still be alive. I was hours too late.

Mrs Barker looked terrible the day of the funeral, I hardly knew her.

As she walked past me on the way out of the cemetery, she stopped and looked up at me. Hers was a face bewildered, and a mind completely shattered by the tragedy of her husband's death. For the ten thousandth time I wished I was ten years older. I longed for some small way to comfort her in her sorrow. She went to move on, then stopped again and said, 'Thank you for the flowers and the help and everything.'

Later, I thought of the great splayed footprints going down through the red mud. I guess he just wanted to admire his dam in the moonlight. He had been wearing his gumboots. And I thought of her, when she had stopped to speak to me, and of how small and neat her ankles and feet were. I don't know why people think of odd things like that at such odd times.

As I had squelched through the mud to drag him out, I'd been pretty careful where I had stepped, so no one else would see the other neat little footprints beside his.

A Matter of Priority

THE DAY JOHNNY LUCAS pulled in the big cod must have been about the hottest for the whole summer, and it had been pretty hot since well before Christmas.

It would have been about the last week of the school holidays, and I went over to Johnny's place to see what he was doing. As he wasn't doing anything in particular, we decided to go on down to the river for a swim, and just more or less from habit took a couple of fishing lines with us. We knew there would be nothing biting on such a clear, hot day, except perhaps a cod that might be tempted with a yabbie, provided we could get a line down into deep water.

There was deep water along there, quite close to the edge of the river, and we reckoned we knew all the likely spots. When I think back on that particular day, it seems as though I can still feel the sun beating down on my shoulders and back with an intensity like a physical weight pressing me down against the hot, sandy ground.

We crossed the road that divided the high land from the irrigated flat, 'The Swamp' we always called it. The sun's heat raised a steaminess from the damp, lush pasture, intensifying the pressure. The swamp could be irrigated directly from the river, producing an almost tropical growth right through the summer months. You could almost hear the rye grass and clover growing as you walked through it. It was hot, and it was only the thought of the cool water at the end of our walk that kept us going.

Had we been asked to walk half that distance to bring the cows home, we'd have found a dozen excuses for not doing it. What with the heat and the impending doom of school starting the next week, neither of us felt much like talking, apart from an occasional remark such as expressing our intention of staying in the water until it was time to go to stinking school.

We kept a couple of yabbie nets in the channel near the river bank. The somewhat over-ripe mutton shank had coaxed enough yabbies into one of them so we could bait a few hooks. We tied our lines together to give us enough length to reach deep water.

Johnny's dad had an old rowing boat tethered under the willows growing along the water's edge, and having secured one end of our line to a convenient branch, we rowed out to the end of the line and let the sinker take it into what we hoped was a cod family's summer residence.

The willows were in full leaf and it was deliciously cool in their shade. The slow moving river never became warm more than a few inches down, and when we lowered ourselves cautiously into the water, we were soon gasping at the sudden cold that contrasted so sharply with the heat of the day. It certainly brought us to life, and we were soon yelling and splashing like a couple of maniacs, with all thoughts of school washed from our mind.

I don't think I ever headed for the river without my mother saying in her quiet way, 'Be careful, and don't go into the deep water,' but as soon as we hit the water, we'd head for the centre and soon have fifty or sixty feet of Old Man Murray under us. Anyway, you could drown just as easily in six feet of water as sixty, and we both knew we were drown-proof.

'Hey Johnny, remember the day you got your foot caught in a snag near the landing?'

'Crikey, I thought I was a goner that day, Fergie. Just as well I wasn't by myself.'

'Yeah, I was scared when you took so long to come up, lucky for you I found you so easy.'

Johnny sloshed a handful of water in my eyes and said, 'Aw, I'd have got out, you can't drown me. Come on, I'll race you back to the boat.'

I beat him back, but had to grab him by the ankle and then push his head under to do it. Between coughing and spluttering, he threatened me with all sorts of terrible vengeance, but as I told him, I had no reason to worry because he'd never catch me anyway. We dragged ourselves back into the boat and had a long and serious discussion about all the things we'd do if we didn't have to go back to school, and considered various means of ridding the world of teachers.

At ease in the boat, with the branches of the willows reaching down until they rested on the water, we were in a different world to the one we had walked through an hour earlier. In the cool of the shade, it was easy to forget the heat of the sun. Stillness and silence were all around us, and even the pleasure of splashing in the water had taken second place to the pleasure of just loafing there with our imaginations running riot. We had run out of nonsense to prattle about and were at peace with the world.

Johnny, as always, was a little more wide awake than I, so it was he who first noticed the line move. 'Hey, Fergie, look,' he said, lazily indicating the general direction of the springy branch to which the line was tied.

The line was tightening gently, but strongly. It bent slightly with the strength of the pull. This wasn't the sudden strike of a fast moving bream; we knew there was no hurry to get to the line. Nevertheless, we were quickly upright with the excitement that every angler knows when something worthwhile shows an interest in the bait. With a quick push on the nearest tree, Johnny sent the boat moving towards the line. He grasped it firmly, saying as he did so, 'It's a whale, Fergie. It must weigh a ton.' His voice was high with excitement.

I joined him in the front of the boat, a safe enough move for a pair of lightweights like us. Taking hold of the line, I could feel the strength of the fish's pull, and knew that Johnny couldn't be much more than three-quarters of a ton out in his estimate of weight.

In my off-balance position, I had to make a fast grab at the side of the boat to stay aboard. With cod, you never know just how big it is until it comes into view. Some are so docile you can almost lead them home to the frying pan with no fight at all.

This one simply wanted to keep going firmly in the other direction, and was probably puzzled and annoyed at the restraint we had placed on him. The line was a good stout one. In those days, we knew nothing of sophisticated rods and reels with light weight nylon line. As Johnny said, 'You could leg rope a damn cow with it.' We had no spare line to play out, so I unhitched the boat, and it moved gently in the direction of the pull for a few feet when the cod decided that more would be accomplished if we all pulled together, and turned towards us. Johnny began to pull in the slack, and the line began to coil neatly in the bottom of the boat. This is a good habit for a line fisherman, as it can run out again without tangling – usually.

The fish was in no great hurry, and all we had to do was take in slack as we led it towards the boat. With about twenty feet of line between us and our prey, it surfaced and we saw it for the first time. The great ugly head was momentarily clear of the water, it looked huge. Old Jack Svenson had a forty pounder in his boat one day, and it wasn't as big as ours. I was sure of it.

We forgot to keep the line taut for a couple of seconds as we stared unbelieving at it. The cod must have felt that it was free of the pull of the hook and it turned rapidly, diving at the same time. The wet line slid through my fingers, and losing my balance, I stepped back with my right foot, fair into the centre of the neat coils that were quickly uncoiling themselves, as if they had come magically alive. At the same time, Johnny was trying to get a good grip on the line again, but my clumsy actions were not making things at all easy for him. As he lunged forward, determined that the fish would be landed at any cost, we met solidly, shoulder to shoulder, amidships.

Unfortunately for me, I was floundering on one leg in a state of near panic, and trying to free the other leg from the tightening tangle of line, with the result that I suddenly hit the water in a pretty good racing dive. I suppose I instinctively tightened my grip on the line, and instead of a shallow dive, I went deep, helped along by the fish that no longer had any wish to be led tamely home.

The boat had drifted out from the willows and now had a good twenty feet of water under it. Both my legs were well entangled by now, and I could not have let go of the line, or the fish, if I'd wanted to. In fact, it was the cod that was leading me back to his home now, and had led me between the branches of a waterlogged tree, twelve or fifteen feet below the surface. Sheer panic took over completely, and it was only the fact that I was normally as much at home in the water as any water rat that I managed to hold the bit of air that remained in my lungs. My wildly kicking legs were, by now, in a tight tangle of sunken tree and stout fishing line, and I'd lost all interest in angling. In my panic, I tugged at the cord with both hands and managed to snag myself even more securely. At this depth the water was really cold and not much light penetrated. I was scared, and my chest hurt, but I still struggled to free myself.

A sudden loosening of the line enabled me to to disentangle my left leg, but my head was trying to burst, and Whiskers Blake the wrestler had a scissors hold on my chest. Then there was something tugging at my arm, and I vaguely realised that Johnny was down there with me. I still have nightmares of the next couple of seconds. I had his throat in both my hands before I blacked out.

The next minute or two must have been the busiest Johnny had ever spent, and I only have his word about what took place, so I'll quote him: 'Well I cut you loose, and dragged you up.'

When I came to, I was face down on the damp, steamy ground, just clear of the water, with Johnny forcing my lungs to work. I said in deep appreciation, 'Get off – gasp – my back – gasp – so I can breathe.'

Then he was talking and laughing and crying all at once, and every time I tried to get up or say anything, he gave me a whack on the ear, but whether it was intentional, or just a reflex action after my attempt to throttle him, I've never known for sure.

'You stupid, clumsy dope. You shouldn't be allowed within a mile of water. You'd drown if I wasn't here to look after you. Why did you try to choke me? I nearly dropped the knife, and you tried to tear my hair out, and stuck your fist halfway down my throat.'

After every few words I got a slap, first on one ear, then on the other, but I was too tired to resist.

'If you tell anyone what happened, I'll drag you back into the river and leave you there, because we wouldn't be able to come to the river again, and I can swim even if you can't, and I can catch fish, so promise not to tell.'

My head was ringing from the near drowning and the pounding Johnny was dealing out. When I suddenly elbowed him just above the hip bone, he decided to shut up and let me get up, if I could.

I tried to stand, and decided to rest awhile. In spite of the heat of the sun I was cold and shivering, and I sat with my aching head in my shaking hands for a few minutes, while the full realisation of what Johnny had done for me sank into my spinning brain.

At last I got up, and saw that Johnny had gathered together our clothes, and what was left of of our fishing tackle – a few yards of tangled cord. As he came up to me I looked at him and felt shy and awkward as I held out my hand to him. He took it. 'Thanks,' I said, and he grinned.

Neither of us felt very bright by the time we'd walked home. Gee, it was hot.

Neither of us mentioned the fish, though we must have been thinking about it as we went along in silence. Just before we reached Johnny's house, he said, 'Don't tell.' So I didn't. I knew my mum and dad wouldn't let us go again if they knew.

'Hello boys,' said Johnny's mother. 'There's a jug of lemon in the cool safe and cake in the cupboard. Was it nice in the water?'

Johnny looked at me and grinned. I'd run right out of grin.

'Aw, beaut mum,' said Johnny. 'Fergie tried to drown me, and we hooked the biggest cod I've ever seen.' Mrs Lucas knew he was only joking and said nothing.

'It was too big to carry home. I'll bet it weighs fifty or sixty pounds. I've gill tied it under the boat. I'll get Dad to go down after tea and get it. Gee, it's a whopper.' I stared at him open-mouthed, because

I suddenly knew he was telling the truth.

'Johnny, you shouldn't tell such stories.'

'But it's dinkum Mum. Isn't it Ferg?'

I managed to say 'It's true all right, Mrs Lucas.'

'See, its that long and its head's as big as mine and it's mouth's as big as Fergie's.'

I wanted to go home, and told Mrs Lucas, I'd better be going.

As we went out together, Johnny said, 'Gee, it took some landing.' I put my hands in a choking position for the second time that day. He only grinned.

When we got outside, I said, 'How did you catch it again after you got me out?'

'What a prize blasted fisherman you'd make. The biggest fish either of us ever saw, and you tried to lose it. I tied it up *before* I cut you loose, you dope.'

Mad

THERE ARE VARIOUS FORMS of madness, each having its own degree of risk, either to the victim or to those around him. Most of my family, especially the male members, had a broad streak of insanity running through them. Fortunately, it only struck at certain times of the year, but when it did, no one was really safe, and everyone felt the effects.

It was somewhat frightening to see a reasonably sane family completely jolted out of its normal, steady work-a-day existence, all in the space of a few days. It was not confined just to the immediate family. Uncles, cousins, in-laws and close friends were also affected. It coincided with the commencement of the cricket season. Through winter and early spring, we would be pursuing a peaceful, humdrum way of life, and then ...

The ground between the apple trees would have been cleaned, freshly turned and freed of weeds. The blossom on the plum trees would have grown to hard little green nobs. The last danger from frost was gone from the vines, and whammo ... some insane young 'un would say, 'Anyone want to bowl me a few?'

It wouldn't be quite right to say we actually had a cricket club, but I knew for a fact that when I stood in front of the wicket, eyes glued on my antagonist's bowling arm, bat poised, I was the very image of Bill Woodfull. There was that same look of complete concentration – stance correct yet relaxed, ready to move my left foot to that position for positive attack, or my right for impregnable defence. Here I was, the copybook cricketer and sportsman, capable of carrying on, in spite of the terrifying onslaught by the opposition's demons, as wickets fell around me.

For the last few months, the frightening figure pounding down to the bowler's wicket had been my elder brother and almost sane workmate. He was now a hated rival, bent on my annihilation.

The bat in my hands had been carefully and religiously anointed with oil last autumn, had hibernated in peace and darkness for the cold, wet months, and now became a living, flaming sword of devastation. Its destiny was to destroy the power of the enemy, and despatch his leathery projectile into the creek.

Poor mum, she knew that we'd be late for the evening meal for weeks on end. That dinner, so lovingly prepared, would be bolted down without us even tasting it or appreciating it, just so we could dash out again to the fray, until the encroaching shades of evening made it too dangerous to stand up to even the spin attack.

Various uncles and cousins around the district played with different teams, and we competed against them from time to time. My own family was split in two, with my parents trying to share their loyalties between the Valley Rovers and the Woods Warriors.

It was also a bit embarrassing, trying to fit four of the Kunz brothers into one team, but equally worrying for the scorer when two were batting, one bowling and Bert, the family wicket-keeper, was crouched over the stumps.

What a divided house we were on the night following a Valley versus Woods game, with Mum trying to keep the peace, and Dad laying down the law as to what we should have done to a particular delivery that had claimed a wicket, or how 'keeper Bert had stood too far back for bowler George.

'You looked as though you were scared of the ball, and George wasn't fast enough to hurt a fly.'

I pulled up my shirt and said, 'Just as well for the fly that he wasn't sitting on my ribs when I stopped that one,' as I tenderly caressed the bruise.

'What the hell do you think the bat's for?' roared Dad, full of no sympathy at all. 'No batsman worth a rotten apple gets bruised ribs, if he knows how to handle his bat, especially against easy bowling like George was trundling down. In my day, we wouldn't even notice a bruise like that.'

'How did you get bruised? Didn't you have a bat?'

'Don't get smart with me, boy. We had real bowlers to stand up against. Even now, George couldn't bust me in the ribs.'

'It's still daylight, Dad, do you want me to trundle down a few?' said George, and in ten seconds flat, Mum and the girls had the house to themselves, and Dad was showing us the right way to hook and pull.

'Well, I suppose I have slowed down a bit,' said Dad, 'and you'd have me in a bit of trouble if you bowled straight and twice as fast.'

I felt my ribs again, but kept the thought to myself that that was about the pace and line he'd been bowling during the game.

'The light's not good for fast bowling, give the ball to Frank, he needs plenty of practice.'

So, I'd say nothing about 'four-for-twenty' and roll over a few leg breaks with a wrong'un here and there for good measure. I must admit that he still knew which way the ball was going to turn, and how much, as well as what to do with it when he got it. In thirty-odd years of batting he had learned a thing or two, and we had learned a thing or two from him, as well.

The big event of the season for us was the annual 'Kunz versus The Rest' picnic game. From the multitude of relatives, the difficult factor was, who to leave out and still keep the peace. Bert was a certainty, as no one could keep as well as he, and George was always sure of his place because of his speed. My batting and last ditch second emergency leg spinners made my position in the team reasonably secure. So eventually, the team would be picked, with something like half-a-dozen twelfth men.

The opposing team would be picked from the several clubs in the district, with an occasional ring-in, which, on one disastrous occasion, turned out be an interstate visitor who made the test team the following season. What he did to us boosted his confidence by no small degree. I scored a six off him – my only hit for the game – it took him two deliveries to warm up.

Well, 'The Rest' mostly did not know us very well or were willing to risk life, limb or reputation by joining in the fun. There was always a certain amount of gamesmanship, not that any of us would stoop to bad sportsmanship or anything like that, we were all such friendly, big-hearted people, and the opposition were our guests after all.

There was always a happy picnic atmosphere, with plenty to eat and drink. The non-playing members of the family were excellent hosts, but woe-betide a member of the home team who was caught with a glass in his hand while the game was on. On the other hand, it would have been a gross discourtesy not to offer refreshment to our guests from the very moment of arrival, and not one of them was going to be able to complain that we were lacking in hospitality.

Each year the day was more or less a repetition of the previous one, and there is no real point in going into lengthy details about the statistics of individual performances, but you can be sure it was a day to remember, and our guests were never in any doubt as to how seriously the Kunz crowd took their cricket.

Win, lose or draw, the highlight of the day was the fun and nonsense that followed far into the night, with a dance in the barn-like structure that gloried in the name of sports pavilion.

Maybe the floor was a little rough and somewhat uphill and down dale. Perhaps the accordion was not what you'd expect at the Trocadero, but no one was ever heard to complain that it was a dull evening. Cricket madness overflowed, and we were never left in doubt, by the numerous self-appointed coaches and advisors, how we could have improved our game. Dad's booming voice could be heard telling all and sundry how he had belted the daylights out of the great Clarrie Grimmett who had been a ring-in at some previous game. 'No one had the sense to recognise him except me, and I'd seen him play so often I knew every trick in his box. There's a bowler you could well pattern yourself on, young Frank.'

'If you could belt him around, then I must be better than him,' I came back at him.

'Look, son, it's bright moonlight and nearly midnight, but you can come out to the wicket now, and I'll bet you the price of a ticket to every day of the fourth Test Match that you can't bowl me, or even get one past me.'

Dad grabbed a bat and threw a ball to me, and like the idiots we were, there was a rush by a dozen or more of us out onto the moonlit oval.

Five minutes later, the rest of them were still there demonstrating

Grimmett leg spinners, and I was back in the hall, happy in the knowledge that I could see every ball of the forthcoming Test Match, and telling Dad how much better Miller and Lindy were than the quickies of his time. I was looking forward to seeing them bowl, especially as it would be at Dad's expense.

It was weeks after the Test Match that I found out that Dad had bought my tickets well before he made the wager with me.

Gradually, the flannelled fools in the moonlight realised the extent of the stupidity of their efforts out in the centre, and wandered back as the party broke up. Another day's cricket and its aftermath had come to an end.

In the fullness of time, the season also came to an end, and forgotten or neglected tasks again received attention. Flannels were put into mothballs and bats anointed and sent to their resting places for the winter. Peace, and some degree of normality, pervaded the home and the orchard. Mum sighed with relief in the knowledge that the dinner cooking in the oven would be eaten and appreciated by a hungry family after a hard day's work. She loved to see us all sit down together, to enjoy a meal without talking or arguing about cricket.

As she went to the door to call us, there came an ominous, heart-pounding thump-thump-thump from down by the shed. George's voice rang out in the evening air, 'Come on Frank, see if you remember how to kick a football.'

Oh, madness upon madness.

Poor Chris

KATE WAS LIKE THAT. It didn't matter how low I felt after going through what Mum always called, one of my brown moods – and brown was no exaggeration – Kate could snap me out if it with a word.

I'd been going to old Carl for nearly three years, and even though I'd learned much more from him during that time than if I had been taking lessons from any other teacher, he'd get the idea that I wasn't trying. The great thatch of white hair would bristle with anger or frustration, and the beautifully modulated speech would take on a slight hint of his boyhood German, instead of his 'Posh, Oxford Pommy sort of accent', as Alec described it. 'Harmoniques – harmoniques – you're just too lazy, you jump from note to note like a sparrow hopping from branch to branch, and its twittering is better music than you'll ever make. Put away your violin boy before you torture the very spirit out of it – go learn the bagpipes of your heathen ancestors, you haven't the soul of a musician.'

Dad, and all the Ferguson forebears, would have been up in arms at this insult to the Highlanders and their beloved pipes and pibroch.

In all fairness to Carl, this wouldn't happen until long after the lesson should have been over. It was his quick and sure way of terminating the day's tuition. I should have known him well enough by this time not to take it so much to heart, and later on I realised how tired he must have been of my weary wailing, and how he longed to be left alone to his own, real music.

After the lesson I would dash off, looking as though I wouldn't slow down before I'd reached home, only to stop a few yards down the road and sneak back to listen for a while, just in case he started to play some of his wonderful gypsy dances. It was then I realised how little I knew. And whether he played for a few minutes, which was mostly the case, or for an hour or more, I couldn't leave while he still played. Often I've stayed there shivering in the cold of an evening while he wove a spell of enchantment around me with his impeccable bowing.

My mother would remark on the lateness of the hour, and I would say, 'Mr Wagner was trying to teach me a difficult piece, then he showed me how it was done – I'll never be able to play like that.' Then the brownness of frustration would settle over me, and I'd go off to bed, to lie there listening to Alec snoring while he dreamed of whichever was his favourite young lady at that particular time – and several others as well. What a generous fellow he was, sharing himself with all the pretty girls around the district.

I'd go over in my mind the way I played, and the harshness of Carl's words, then despair at the purity of sound that came from his playing. I was too young and stupid to realise how much he had come to mean to me, or what it meant to him to be able to give to me, even a little of his love and knowledge of music. After all, he wasn't exactly what you would call, lavish in his praise. Sometimes he would say, 'That was better, Ian', but in such a way that I felt it couldn't have been any worse.

Youngsters sleep, even when they think they have insurmountable problems, and if the bad mood persisted through breakfast, and followed me out of the house on the way to school, most times it was Kate who I met first, and her cheery, 'Don't worry, Fergie. You look like a Scotsman that lost a shilling and found a button. Och mon, buttons can be useful, Laddie.' Then she would chatter and tease, and I'd realise that the sun was shining, and it was getting close to the end of the second term, with holidays just around the corner, so if winter goes, spring is nearly behind us too, and my last year at school finished and …

Yes, that was it, Dad said I could please myself whether I went to high school or not. He reckoned that I was old enough to make that decision myself, and I hadn't the wisdom to see the value of study. There was my violin, and the few shillings I could make playing for dances, and not only on Saturdays, once I had left school. Perhaps I was wiser then than I am now. Learning doesn't always bring wisdom, and it is possible to be wise while not being well read. But I'm no great philosopher.

Kate was determined to go to high school in the town and then get an arts degree, somehow or other, even if it took her the rest of her life. She was that determined.

At that age, I still looked upon her as a playmate and friend from next door, and never in my wildest imaginings thought of her as ever being a woman, or even a female, I suppose. I guess this is the normal attitude of school kids. Kate and I were closer than most brother and sister pairs, and saw nothing unusual in being together. I think we gained a lot by doing our homework together of an evening all those years, because we were always yards ahead of the rest of the small class at school. Even the friendly, teasing, competitive spirit she adopted, spurred me on to at least equal her high standard some of the time, though I could never outclass her.

Now I'm old. I sit here in my study, dreaming of her loveliness, and what has gone by, trying to put my scattered thoughts into some sort of chronological order. My thoughts, however, hop around from year to year, like Carl's twittering sparrows and my long neglected 'harmoniques' – but I still have his violin – and there I go, jumping the years again.

There are not many philosophers at thirteen years of age. My biggest problem at the time was trying to master Old Crazy Carl's lessons. This in fact was the only ambition I had, not so much with the idea of becoming a great musician, but because Carl seemed to expect it of me. That, and the bit of Scots stubbornness I had inherited from the Fergusons, had determined me to fiddle or bust.

It must have been around this time, I suppose, that Mum's brother, Uncle George, and Aunt Christine, moved in on us from parts unknown, with no definite plans for the future, as far as I could work out. They were the aristocrats of the family – except to aristocrats – and were far and away too superior to toil in the cow yard, or do any work around the place, but were always available for advice on any subject, whether it was wanted or not.

They were a fair bit younger than Mum and Dad, and Chris was an up-to-the-minute flapper type, going gaily through life, as though acting a part on stage. George, on the other hand, was as dull as he was lazy – an honest to goodness free-loader. The family must have won him in a raffle; the mind boggles as to what the second prize must have been. Chris insisted that she was too young to be called Aunt, so, to Mum's great disapproval, she was Chris to all of us.

She was a bright spot in our lives, even though she never failed to shock our parents with her modern ways. Cigarettes, beer and wicked jokes were each most important in her life. We thought she was beautiful, and she was.

One day she wanted to climb onto the haystack, so Jim obligingly held the ladder for her, and up she went. When nearly to the top she squealed in her very best stage manner, 'Oh, Jim, I can see everything from here.' Jim looked up and said, 'Yeah, me too.'

They never seemed to be short of money to spend on the necessities of life, except such mundane items as food and lodging. Not that Dad would have accepted it. Like all good Scots he was careful with his money, but without a mean bone in him.

It must have been an awful strain on our guests, having to put up with country fare. They were complete urbanites, but as Chris said to Mum one day, 'Darling, it's so essential to stagnate a little now and then, and dear George does need the rest.' Dad said, 'He'd take the damn lot if you'd let him,' but only so us boys could hear him. We never found out from what earnest endeavours he was resting, but it was obvious that he was going to be well rested by the time he left Masons Flat.

There were times when Chris wished that George hadn't recovered from whatever it was that he needed rest. Once was when she first met Brian Schwartz. He was the eldest and handsomest of the Schwartz family, also the shyest with anyone he didn't know very well. Kate used to tease him about, 'Fergie's beautiful Aunty that likes to dance with you all night and find excuses to send dear George out to the car to get her cigarettes, Darling', all said in Chris's most flapperish manner.

Uncle George didn't care to dance, but Chris was never short of partners. She flirted shamelessly with every male, married or single, young or old, and they all loved it – except perhaps Brian, though he didn't exactly run away, but once or twice he seriously considered it. She was quite an accomplished pianist and played all the popular jazz music of the twenties.

'Ian darling, don't tell me you play real music as well as the dreadful stuff that weird old man makes you learn.' She hadn't met Carl when she said that, but when she eventually did, she nearly swooned into his arms when he clicked his heels, and bowed over her hand. 'Oh, what a divine old gentleman, you never said he was anything like that. Naughty Alec even called him Crazy Carl. Now, how can I get rid of dear George.'

George gave a sad coughing sound that was, for him, a hearty laugh, 'Oh really, Christine – you really shouldn't ah, um, you know.'

'Dear George thinks I'm joking, but your Carl is so suave, so urbane, he must be a count that had to leave home. Oh Darling, I wonder if he had to fight a duel, and if she was worth it. Would you challenge him to a duel George dear if he ... ?'

'Hummff – chuff, really you are, frummph, you know, really.' Uncle George had a wonderful depth of repartee.

I must admit that I enjoyed Chris's real music, and if she didn't like hearing me practice Carl's dreadful stuff, she never said so. We had some great times playing jazz, and we even decomposed some of the dreadful stuff to dance tempo – quickstep and charleston.

Well, Carl enjoyed dance music. 'The best dance musicians in the world had to learn to play, boy, and they learned it the way you do, with years of study and practice, and you'll do no harm playing dance music either, as long as you do practice. When you don't, you can find yourself another teacher,' and he'd wag his scary mane like a hairy metronome. Then I'd go over and over a line of music until I felt like finding another teacher, like Chris – at least she was pretty.

We'd giggle over my mistakes, and she'd make me feel embarrassed by kissing me on the cheek and calling me 'Darling Ian.' I never said I didn't like it. She even smelt nicer than Carl, and her bobbed hair was smooth and shiny. 'Ian, sweet, you're blushing,' and I knew it, so we'd both giggle again.

I really think she would have got rid of dear George if she could have got around Brian. There were times when Brian wished there wasn't a Dear George. But there was, and as far as Brian was concerned, that was the end of it, and there was no beginning.

I never gave the matter any thought at the time, but looking back from half a century away, I feel that there was more than I realised in the dances that Chris and Brian had together. One thing I do know, Chris never giggled or prattled on in her stage performance voice when she danced with him. You can see more from up on the little stage in the corner of the hall than you can from the dance floor. No one ever danced better than those two.

So maybe she was the reason that, years later, Brian said, 'Sure, I'm not the courtin' type.' He might have seen more behind her make-believe nonsense that she presented to the world-at-large than we realised. Even if she had been prepared to go a little further than a few dances, Brian wasn't the type to be led on, or to lead her on either.

That, then, was the end of the romance that never was. It's impossible to remember how long they stayed with us, but eventually, Chris must have felt that they had stagnated for long enough, and to the relief of all the females at Masons, and the mixed feelings of the mere males, they moved on. I never saw her again, and Mum only saw her twice. Once when she attended George's funeral.

They had bought a smart little roadster, which George never drove, and on a drive in the Adelaide hills they stopped to admire the view from Windy Point. Chris got out of the car, which, unfortunately, rolled several hundred feet down an extremely steep slope. There have been solid guard rails there ever since.

The next time Mum saw her was a few weeks later. Chris seemed to be standing up to her sudden widowhood quite well. 'I looked absolutely ghastly in black, darling, and dear George wouldn't want me to mope around.'

Poor Chris.

The End

SEBASTIAN CORNFOOT IS A most unlikely name, you must admit, and as it happened, he was a most unlikely gentleman. He was a small, quiet, skinny little man, and people were inclined to consider him a bit of a crank. I did.

Since then I've gained some wisdom and am now slow to criticise another fellow's religious views just because they seem a bit way-out and different from my own. Goodness knows, my own views, though accepted by many, have been ridiculed for centuries, and so it will continue world without end, maybe.

For several years, to my knowledge, Seb told everyone with whom he had contact that the world, as we know it, would end at midnight on Friday, the thirteenth of July, nineteen hundred and thirty-four. Well, somewhere it's midnight, and the year doesn't really matter much, as it's long past, and no one cares whether he was correct or not.

Mr and Mrs Cornfoot lived in a bit of a shack down the road a piece from our place, and they scratched out a sort of an existence growing and selling vegetables and, in season, lush strawberries, whose flavour tickles the taste buds of my memory to this day. Seb would pick up a bit of casual work here and there, and even though he was a bit weird – there I go again – he was an honest man who, I believe, considered the job, however menial, more important than the remuneration.

He and his wife belonged to some exclusive group that went under the name of Job's Followers. Patience was his by-word, and no-one ever heard him complain about the trials and tribulations of life, even when they were visited upon him in many and varied forms.

This short chronicle of his history is not an attempt to promote his canonisation, even though, in his own little way, he may well have been a modern day Saint Francis. Horses or cows that were stubborn or fractious with the rest of us, became docile under his strong but gentle hands. I suppose it was because they sensed our own impatience that made them hard to handle. They knew instinctively that they had nothing to fear from him, with his easy approach and his quiet, soothing voice.

I'm afraid that us school kids were not above baiting him. Two or three of us, when passing his garden on the the way home from school, would stop and give him a bit of cheek. 'How much longer have we got, mister?'

Old Seb would lean on his spade and say, 'There's more than a year to go yet, lads, so you won't get out of this year's exams, and you'll still have to go back to school after Christmas.' He'd say it seriously, but not without humour, and we would feel as if our bit of cheek had backfired on us. Then, as likely as not, he would give us a short homily or a story from the Old Testament, and even if we were not much of Christians, we would stay and listen to him, perhaps because of the child-like simplicity of his manner. 'Well boys, the garden won't dig itself, so I can't stand here talking all day. Here, take these few carrots, and if you hurry, you might be home in time for your mothers to cook them.'

We didn't realise that he gentled us just as he would have a nervous horse, and then got rid of us with a gift.

'Thank you, Mr Cornfoot.'

'You're welcome, boys. Come back for another conversation some time,' and we would go on our way feeling a bit ashamed that our only purpose in stopping was to annoy him.

Mrs Cornfoot had not been in the best of health for quite a number of years, and no one was all that surprised when she died after a few days in hospital. Seb accepted her passing without complaint, but was noticeably saddened at his loss. From then on, I'm sure, he never purchased any new clothes, probably realising that his existing wardrobe would last unto the end of time.

He continued to attend services in the little timber and iron chapel that he and his fellow Jobians had built in the town a few miles up river, and if any of the neighbours were sick or needed a hand, Seb was always the first to offer assistance, as usual.

I asked Dad one day, 'Do you think old Seb is a bit barmy?' To which I was told that to me he was *Mister* Cornfoot, and what proof did I have that I wasn't a bit barmy, whatever that meant. 'Johnny Lucas said you were a flamin' drongo when you started to learn the violin, did that mean he thought you were a bit barmy?' But Dad could tick me off, and I'd see the twinkle in his eye, so I knew that he was too charitable to say, 'Well he is a bit off.' Besides Dad and Seb were pretty good friends, and I didn't think Dad was a bit barmy; even when he tried to imitate Harry Lauder.

Kate Schwartz flared up like a bushfire in a whirlwind when I said, 'The old coot's crazy.' She wouldn't let me come over to her place to do my homework that night, but I still got as much of it correct as she did, even if it wasn't as neat.

One day, Mum sent me to Seb's place for a cabbage and said to ask him if he was well. He was sitting on the front verandah in the late afternoon sun reading his Bible, and asked me to sit down as he had just made a lemon drink, and there was plenty for us both. He asked about school and spoke about my violin lessons. The violin was something of an oddity then, so maybe I was too.

'Mr Cornfoot, how do you know the world is going to end?' I asked him. There was amusement in the look he gave me, because he knew that, with the exception of a handful of the members of his sect, no one took him seriously on that particular prophecy. This is roughly the reply he gave.

'Well, Ian, on several occasions during my life, God has seen fit, for reasons of his own, to reveal to me, events that would take place, not only involving me and people around here, but also on a national and, on one occasion, an international scale. I spoke of these things to other people and was told I was going loony, but when they eventually took place, they preferred to keep quiet on the subject. Then, when I started seeing quite clearly the date, July thirteenth of this year, I knew it was to be a day of great significance.

'I have prayed a lot about this revelation during the last few years and, through prayer, I have long since come to the conclusion that, once again, I have been given the gift of prophecy. Believe me, my boy, it's a gift I'd much rather be without, if the choice were mine, but like Job in the Old Testament, I have learnt to accept that which is sent, and not complain about it.'

Then he gave me that smile that seemed so out of character with his normal seriousness. It seemed, when he smiled like that, that inside the man there was a great wealth of happiness that he wanted to share with us all, and that he was indeed close to God, as he saw Him.

That was probably the longest time I ever took to buy a cabbage, if 'buy' is the right word, as he refused to take anything for it, or for the few late strawberries that he and I collected.

Mum wouldn't believe me when I said that we had been talking all that time. 'Whatever were you talking about?'

'Aw, nothing much – just school and things – he's not really barmy.' Mum said that she had never said he was.

Well, Seb's clothes began to look as if they wouldn't see the distance, and Mum asked him one day if he had any mending he'd like done. Seb chuckled with amusement and said, 'I don't know what a man should wear to meet his Maker, do you?'

'Oh dear, I wish you wouldn't say things like that, you sound as though you are looking forward to what you say is going to happen,' said Mum.

'Well, to me, the hereafter is much more exciting and desirable than the present, so why be unhappy about it?' was Seb's reply.

I always had a fair sort of imagination, and Seb seemed so convinced that the end was in view, that I hardly knew what to think about his prophecy.

If you know anything about mid-winter on the Murray, you will know that there are more desirable chores than yarding up cows in the dark on a frosty morning. Nevertheless, it was with some relief that I greeted the morning of July the fourteenth, and my waking thoughts were that he was just a barmy old coot after all.

It was cold. The grass crackled like dry toast, and my ears tingled with the bite of the frost in the calm air. The cows didn't want to get up out of their hollows in the sandy ground. I stamped about and wished there were no such things as cows and frosty mornings, until I realised that, had Seb been correct in his prophecy, there wouldn't be. It didn't really hurt me to get up early on Saturdays to give Alec a sleep in. I was so busy hunting up lazy cows, and taking an object lesson in Job's and Seb's patience, that I soon forgot to feel cold. After all, there is a certain beauty in frosty mornings, if you cared to look around once it was light enough. The trees along the river were floating in a little sea of low-lying mist, and as the sun rose, the whole morning became a glory of blue, gold and white. So much for Seb's prophecy.

After breakfast, Dad said he would go and see if Seb wanted anything from the town. There was no sign of him around, and since he didn't answer Dad's knock, he went in – no one ever locked their doors, our key had been lost for years.

Seb was in bed, eyes closed, at peace with the world. The doctor said that he'd had a heart attack soon after going to bed.

The Spirit of the Snowies

PERHAPS IT'S BECAUSE I'VE always been a bit on the quiet side, not much good at keeping a conversation going, that I have developed a sympathetic ear for anyone with a story to tell. People subconsciously feel that: 'Here's a fellow I can talk to in safety. He won't go telling everyone what I say.' Whatever the reason, I have spent a fair bit of my life listening to the stories of quite a variety of folk. Maybe they knew I was interested. It is a fact that people are interesting if you sit quiet, and let them ramble on.

One of my favourite ramblers was Johnny Lucas's grandfather, whose name was also John, but because of age and rather reserved manner, everyone at Masons Flat addressed him as Mister Lucas. While still a young man, he had come out from Yorkshire, but had retained his delightful north country accent, and I never tired of listening to his reminiscences. He had about him a strong gentleness which gave him an air of old world courtesy, elements of character that he had passed on to his son Charlie to quite a marked degree.

One of my favourite fishing spots was the old wooden landing where the old milk boat, and the even older paddle steamer that supplied the pumping station with coke, would berth.

This particular day, the fish were not hungry, and I wasn't all that interested in them either, so I was leaning back against the bollard-like corner post – a good solid one, some eighteen inches through – when the senior Mr Lucas strolled up, bade me good afternoon, and wondered if I would mind him joining me for a few minutes. He stiff-jointedly took up a similar position to mine at the other corner of the landing, and after a few preliminary remarks on the slowness of the fish, the pleasantness of the day and so on, asked me if I believed in ghosts.

It was one of those clear, warm, blue and white days that made the waterside willows almost burst into leaf while you sat and watched them. In fact, not the sort of day to consider the existence of ghosts. The pair of pelicans I had been watching as they glided so slowly on the calm water a couple of hundred yards upstream were too real and material to even want to think of a vague spirit world. I said, 'No'.

Mr Lucas was such a sound, solid type that I knew I had given him the answer he wanted, so I was quite pleased with myself when he said, 'Most people would have said *no* to that question, Ian, and quite rightly too, because not many have had any evidence that ghosts exist. But, by the same token, I've never met anyone with any proof that they do not.'

The second part of his reply dented my ego a little and I said, 'Then do you believe in ghosts, Mr Lucas?'

That was the wrong thing to say if I wanted his company for only a few minutes. It was also the last remark I made for quite some time as he let his mind reach back over the years to when he was young and footloose, and was trying his hand at trapping dingoes in the wild, rough country of south-eastern New South Wales.

From the southern edge of the Monaro Plains, the hills ran up to the Snowy Mountains; beautiful, broken country accessible only to horsemen, and only experienced ones at that.

The wild dogs had long since developed a taste for mutton and lamb and were not endearing themselves to the hearts of the graziers, so young John decided that he would diminish the packs, and make wages from the bounty paid by the government for their scalps.

He had with him a saddle horse that had more than a turn of speed. His deep chest indicated plenty of strength and staying power. Neither speed nor stamina was needed to stay ahead of the old, black packhorse, which was slow, solid and reliable, with more years behind it than there were ahead. King Coal was the sheet anchor to the unpredictably temperamental Mack, who, in normal circumstances, chose to keep close to his companion. It was Coal, therefore, who wore the hobbles at night, as Mack objected to them to such a degree that he was in danger of doing himself an injury in trying to escape from them.

The two remaining members of the company were a pair of dogs of questionable and completely untraceable parentage. Big, rough-haired brindle brutes, wilder than the dingoes they were trained to hunt, and considerably more dangerous, with courage to attack man or beast, or even each other, at the least provocation. John never went near them without his loaded rifle when they were not muzzled, or were off the leash. Not that they had ever attacked him, but he didn't see any reason in taking risks with them. They seldom barked, and it always seemed to John that they wore an air of superiority, as if they owned him, rather than the reverse. Perhaps the isolation and the loneliness were getting to him a bit.

Although it was late spring, the high tops in the distant west and around to the south, still wore their white winter caps. The southerly wind gave no indication that summer was on its way. The morning had broken clear and cold, and there was more than a hint of frost in the air as John visited his trap line. He marvelled, as he always did on such mornings, at the clearness of the air. In the rising sun, the mountain tops turned pink against the pale blue, and merged with the deeper blues and greys of the lower slopes as, from the deep valleys, wisps of mist rose white, like the smoke of so many campfires.

The traps had yielded a couple of young dingoes, whose scalps would pay for the day's rations, and a large, extremely bad-tempered wombat. John had some difficulty in releasing the third victim, but eventually managed to do so without it suffering anything more than a sore foreleg and a loss of dignity. The damaged foot made its retreating waddle less graceful than usual. At its best, the hairy-nose is not a thing of remarkable beauty, though one cannot but admire its appearance of solid reliability.

The sun was well up by the time he had returned to camp. If a snarling sort of a growl can be called a greeting, then his faithful hounds greeted him most cordially. Coal looked up from his grazing and snickered softly, either to Mack or his rider. The camp was an old slab and bark hut, built by some would-be grazier who had seen the futility of keeping his flocks intact in such rough country, country that can be unkindly bleak and cold in the winter months, and as equally hot and barren in mid-summer. The close proximity of cover for the wild dogs had, no doubt, added to his troubles.

By mid-day a south-westerly had sprung up, and sudden gusts of almost gale force came across the snow-clad tops, bringing heavy rain and hail that reduced visibility to a few yards. The gusts would cease as suddenly as they started, taking the clouds with them and leaving the whole area in bright sunshine for an hour or more.

The past several weeks had yielded a fair swag of scalps. Rations were low, to the point of disappearing altogether, so John decided that he had had enough of dingoes and his own company. Tomorrow, he would break camp early and head for Cooma, which he expected to reach sometime on the third afternoon. For the rest of today and tonight, he would stay as warm and snug as the hut permitted. It was certainly more comfortable indoors, with a fire in the stone fireplace, than it was out in the teeth of the minor blizzard coming in from the Snowies. He had shot a good-sized 'roo the previous evening so the dogs wouldn't go hungry, and any gourmet would enjoy the soup he was looking forward to making from its tail.

The sun set in a blaze of glory, colouring the sky and the mountain tops with an extravagance that would be impossible to capture on canvas. The riot of pinks, through to orange and red, contrasted with the blue, green and gold of the clearing sky. With the setting of the sun, the wind dropped, and silence settled over the scene.

By the light of a hurricane lantern and the flickering fire, John prepared for bed. He opened the leather-hinged door of the shack, made sure that the dogs were securely tethered and the horses close by. Three-quarters of a moon had risen, giving him light enough to see his four companions. One of the dogs gave a friendly snarl, as if to say, 'I'd be at your throat if it wasn't for this chain.' And, as if in answer, a dingo, somewhere off in the direction of the moon, lifted its head and gave full voice in protest at all the indignities heaped upon it and its race since sheep had been introduced to its menu.

In a split second, the chains of both dogs snapped as taut as the strands of wire in a well-strained fence. Mack gave a snort of surprise and reared suddenly. John had heard dingoes howl every night for weeks, and the dogs, if they took any notice at all, would growl and go back to sleep. Yet he had never heard such a piercing, long drawn-out howl, almost a scream, as had come from the throat of the lone wild dog. Perhaps the dead silence after the roughness of the day had exaggerated the sound, or maybe the loneliness of the mountains had stirred his imagination, but why the sudden fierce reaction of the animals? And why were the dogs straining their chains to breaking point – away from the direction of the sound?

John felt the hair at his temples prickle, and there was a creeping sensation in the skin covering his ribs. He returned to the hut and picked up his Winchester rifle. He had spent the last of his shearing cheque from the previous season on the best firearm he could find.

Making sure it was fully loaded, with one in the breach, he was about to leave the hut again and had reached the open door. He froze as the piercing scream again shattered the silence of the hills. With a howl of complete panic, the dogs flew to the extent of their chains, which snapped as though made of cotton. The great beasts kept going, straight at John standing in the lighted doorway. Whether they were going to attack, or were seeking the safety of the cabin, he didn't know, nor did he have much time to decide. As they raced panic-stricken towards the doorway, with one accord they sprang towards him. As he threw himself to the ground, John had time to get off one shot, and one of the dogs dropped to the ground without a sound or a movement, while the other, snapping and snarling, hurtled across his prone figure into the hut, crashing against the back wall.

John sprang to his feet and slammed the door shut. He could hear the animal, completely frenzied and intent on tearing the hut and its contents to pieces. Having secured the door, he became aware that Mack had bolted and was headed for the ranges at full gallop, crashing his way through the undergrowth in his panic to escape from the chaos of mad dogs, howling dingoes and rifle fire. Old King

Coal tried to follow, but the hobbles almost brought him down, and he now stood snorting nervously.

Inside the shack, the wrecker was still at work, and fearing that his belongings would be totally destroyed, John pumped a shell into the breach of the Winchester and pulled open the door. As it swung open, the dog came out at a dead run and made for the hills. The hunter realised that a mad dog among the sheep would be more damaging than the dingoes. He lifted the rifle to his shoulder, took quick aim and fired. He was a good shot.

As he was about to re-enter the hut, he glanced towards the moon, and on a rise, not two hundred yards away, was a black, crouching figure, the size of a man, one arm out-stretched towards him, motionless. He again felt his scalp prickle as the cry of the wild dog once more went echoing across the hills. The sound seemed to come from the crouching figure. John fought the impulse to turn and run, as the animals had, but again he raised the rifle and fired into the threatening intruder, giving no thought to the fact that he might be committing murder. He fired again and again until the magazine was empty, knowing that he couldn't miss at that distance, even by the light of the moon. It hadn't moved.

John didn't know how long he stood watching who or whatever it was, but he did know that he felt fear. Then, when another dingo howled an ordinary salutation to the moon, he came out of his trance, shrugged his shoulders and moved towards his motionless target, but realising that he was out of ammunition, he turned back to the hut.

The lantern hung from a rafter. The fire still burned brightly. The interior of the cabin looked as though a tornado had struck. The bedding had been dragged from the bunk and was in shreds. Flour from the bag, which had been hanging from a hook on the wall, made it look as though the tornado had been followed by a snowstorm.

Dishes and cooking utensils had been swept off the table, which was the only piece of furniture left standing, for the simple reason that its legs were solidly embedded in the earth floor.

Fortunately, his bag of scalps was hanging in a tree some distance away; it did not make for pleasant company in the hut.

John reloaded his rifle and was about to go out, but then thought better of it. Closing the door, he fastened it as securely as its flimsy hinges and latch would permit. He piled the remaining firewood onto the fire and then seated himself on the remains of the bunk facing the door. With the rifle on his knees, and feeling nervous, tired, puzzled and foolish, he waited for morning.

The beginnings of daylight found him still sitting in the same position after a night that was cold, silent and seemingly endless. It seemed to him that the first sound he heard was from his creaking joints when he tried to move. The cold inside the hut made the interior decorations of flour more snow-like than ever.

Once out in the grey morning light, he felt even more foolish when he saw the blackened tree stump, with four fresh bullet holes. Its broken branch, which had been pointing to the open doorway, soon found its way to the fireplace for his morning billy of tea. The carcasses of his dogs and the absence of his saddle horse, gave him sufficient evidence that something strange and unknown had been abroad last night.

Tracks showed that a dingo had trotted past the bullet-riddled stump since the last of yesterday's rain, but the weary trapper had visions of a long hike ahead of him and was not all that interested in dingo tracks, or where they led.

I realised that Mr Lucas had stopped talking and that a lot of warmth had gone out of the sun.

'So, you see, Ian, I don't have any proof that there are any ghosts, and there are times when dogs and horses appear to be more imaginative than people, and they scare for no apparent reason.

'Good old King Coal carried my collection of scalps back to Cooma, and after a long day's walk I was able to borrow a saddle horse from a squatter, but I never saw Mack again.

'I never trapped dingoes again, either.'

Just Kate

Preface

A Package from Scotland

I was surprised and saddened to receive a letter from my uncle's housekeeper informing me that Uncle Ian, my namesake, had died. She said in her letter that the Reverend Ian Ferguson had asked her to forward his journals to me, but because the package was extremely bulky it was travelling by surface mail to save expense.

In due course, a large and sturdy case arrived. It contained several exercise books, and to my surprise, a very old and beautiful violin. The exercise books made very interesting reading.

The Journals

I WAS FIVE YEARS OLD when Dad bought the dairy farm at Masons Flat in 1925. The first thing that came to my attention was the school, which was only a couple of cricket pitches away from the house into which we had moved.

The very first day we were there, two visitors called to see us. One said, 'I'm Sarah, what's yours?'

The other was a black-haired girl, my age, with big brown eyes. She said, 'My mother said I could come in and meet you, but not to stay. I'm Kate.'

The population of Masons in our early years there was just over one hundred, with about thirty on the school roll. Several of the settlers were returned soldiers from the First World War. The town was built beside the Murray River, from which the farms were irrigated. The flat was the shape of an archer's bow, the wood of the bow being the river bank and the string was the road that ran east-west for about three and a half miles.

Eight miles upstream was the town where we did most of our shopping, but the most important shop was a little grocery store, run by Mr Grey, which was also the Masons Flat post office.

A reliable means of transport into town was to beg a ride on the boat that took the milk to the factory. Horse and cart was how we got our milk to the landing. Chariot races were not unheard of, but not at all popular with the poor old nags, especially in the summertime when milk was picked up twice a day.

Mail was also delivered by boat, and was picked up by Mr Grey with his faithful little Pickles and his sulky. Maybe Pickles would not have starred in harness racing, but he gave faithful service for many years; and a bag of chaff clocked up a fair few miles.

Because there were no telephones in those early days, the community contacted the Post-Master General's department with a plea for contact with the rest of world. The response from the PMG was, 'Forward ten applications and we will talk business.'

When only nine applications could be gathered, the PMG adamantly stated, 'Ten, we said.'

Dad and Mum talked it over, and added our name to the list with the result that, in a surprisingly short time, we were linked to anywhere in Australia from nine in the morning to six in the afternoon. Mr Grey at the shop became our resident telephonist. Outside of those hours, an extra charge was made, providing that Mr or Mrs Grey was at home. Our phone number was Masons Flat 3. We got used to the occasional knock on the door and the request, 'Can we use the phone, please.'

From the day I started school, Kate and I shared homework, but it took me many years to fall in love with her.

My other firm friend at that school was Sam. Right from the start, 'Sam and Ian' became one word. We spent most of our spare time together, and as the school years passed we wandered far and wide together, mostly keeping out of mischief, but becoming skilful at not being found out.

Our favourite haunt was the clump of willows that bordered the shallows along the earthen levee. Just a bit upstream from the flat there were some low cliffs, maybe twenty feet above normal water level. I wasn't all that keen on diving in from that height, but it didn't worry Sam. Maybe I had a bit more common sense.

The day was hot and the water cool when he dived in and didn't surface in the expected time. I began to panic and didn't know what to do. After what seemed to be an age he popped up with a grin on his face.

'You stupid drongo,' I said. 'Where were you?'

'Right under your feet.'

'Don't be mad, it's solid rock,' I said.

'That's what I thought too, but there's a hole the size of a forty-four-gallon drum right through into a cave about ten feet across, and the roof is about ten feet above water.'

We swore each other to secrecy, with dire threats of expulsion from our gang of two if the secret ever leaked out.

From then until we became more sensible, it was our secret summer retreat. I didn't think Sam would ever find out that I'd told Kate about it.

Like a great full stop, a couple of hundred yards from the eastern end of the flat was a most impressive pile of granite rocks, and near the rocks stood a neat little limestone cottage. A bloke called Crazy Carl lived there. Sam said that he tortured cats, "Cos I've heard him.'

Not far from the shop stood the Masons Flat Institute Hall, built in 1922. All sorts of wonderful events were held there, including the good old-fashioned Saturday night dances. Mostly, the music was provided by an upright piano. I was about ten years old when I went with my parents to a dance there and Crazy Carl had brought his fiddle.

Because the night was warm, with a full moon shining as bright as day, supper was served outside on a patch of lawn. I was tired, so I'd crawled behind the piano, where I could feel and hear the music, and soon dozed off. I woke to the most beautiful sound I'd ever heard. It was Carl's violin, but it was nothing like the dance music he had been playing earlier. I lay there spellbound until the last note died so softly that to me it was like a golden thread reaching up to the moon.

'That was beautiful, Mr Wagner,' I said.

He was unaware that he'd had an audience. Looking behind the piano he said, 'So, the boy is a musician. Yes?'

'No, Mr Wagner, but if I could play like that I would be.'

He replied, 'It takes many years to become a violinist.'

The crowd was returning by now, and that put an end to our conversation.

Next morning at breakfast, Dad said, 'Did you sleep through supper last night, Ian? That's not like you.'

'No, but I did go to sleep and woke up when Crazy Carl started playing.'

'You mean Mister Wagner, don't you?'

'Yes, Dad. But I waited until he stopped playing, it was so nice.'

'Yes, I heard him. I don't know what it was but it was jolly good.'

So, that was that, until a couple of evenings later when Kate and I were doing our homework. Her dad was in the big chair dozing off and then waking with a start. He made some remark about nothing in particular, just to prove he was awake. I asked him, 'Mr Schwartz, did you hear Mr Wagner playing during suppertime at the dance?'

'Oh yes, that was Liebestraum, composed by a man called Liszt about eighty years ago, very beautiful.'

Mr Schwartz spoke with a slight accent and I'd sometimes heard him and Carl speaking in German.

The Schwartz family were the only Irish Catholic family in Masons Flat. Frank had fallen in love with a beautiful, dark-haired girl of Irish descent who ruled the roost with a gentle touch, much to the obvious contentment of her massive husband. When Mum first asked her what family she had, she said, 'Three boys, three girls and Kate.'

'What do you mean, "and Kate"?'

'Well,' she said, 'at her best she's a real lady and then sometimes she's got more devil than the boys.'

A few days after that dance, Dad said to me, 'I met Mr Wagner at the shop today and he asked me if I thought you would like to learn the violin. Would you?'

'Why would he ask that?' I said.

'He said that any boy that chooses music ahead of supper might also choose music ahead of sport. So, what do you say?'

'Do you mean he would teach me? But why? Can we afford lessons?'

Dad said, 'I asked him that. He reckons if you go for a while and still want to really practice then that would be payment enough.'

The following Saturday morning I went to see Carl. My life changed completely.

We talked for a while and I liked the way we could talk to each other. I'd never been able to talk easily with other adults. I told him that I didn't know if Dad could afford to buy a violin.

He said, 'Your father would be foolish to buy one because you might soon tire of lessons. I have a couple and you could start off with one of them. But you have to take your lessons seriously and not skip practice. I will know if you do.'

So, time went on and the first few months were very difficult. However, Carl had a no-nonsense approach to anything he thought was important. For Carl, music was very important, as was sharing his knowledge and love of music. From Carl I learnt a deep respect for music. I wanted, more than anything, to accept what he had to give. We got on well.

My brother Alex, had an ear attuned to a different kind of music and that was the sweet sound of a well-tuned motor. Dad said, 'Why don't you go and see Joe Morgan in town about a job there? There's no harm in asking.'

When Alex asked Joe for work, Joe said, 'See that heap of scrap in the corner? That's the wreck of a motorbike. Any spare time you have in the next six weeks, come and work on it. If by then you can ride it, it's yours, to get to work. But, you have to pay to register it.'

Alex started at Joe's just a month later. By then I had finished primary school. Sam had started at the high school in town and was making more and better friends, and not just boys.

I stayed on the dairy farm with Dad and was about as good as a man short for the first couple of years. Not having homework to share, I had to find other excuses to call next door at weekends.

Kate was going to the convent school in town, doing her first year at secondary school, staying with an aunt during the week and coming home at weekends. Somehow, the weeks seemed longer.

By the time I was eighteen, I was still finding time to spend an hour or two a week with Carl.

Skinny Watson played piano and had a wild left hand that would have given Fats Waller competition. Sam could beat the hide off a drum. The three of us thought we were better than the Joe Loss Orchestra.

Sadly, I said goodbye to Kate when she entered the convent to be a Josephite nun.

Alex came home from work one day and said, 'I know where there's an A-Model two-seater, it needs a few minor jobs done on it and it's well worth the price they want. The work will cost the price of the parts.'

Nearly all my share of the money from the dance band had gone into my savings. The next day I went to the bank and withdrew a substantial part of my savings; and I became the proud owner of a car. In those days, in South Asutralia, you could get a driving license at sixteen, and I'd been driving Dad's old Chev truck for a couple of years.

Being mobile meant the band could take engagements further afield, and to the objections of Sam and Skinny, I insisted that the car was just as useful as the musicians and so it should get a quarter of the takings.

My visits to Carl had become a bit irregular, more of a social call than a lesson. On the day that turned out to be the last one, he said, 'I can teach you no more, Ian. No, I don't mean you have no more to learn, but I am too old to teach.'

Carl died that night.

The following week a letter came for me from the local solicitor asking me to call on him as soon as possible, which I did the next day, wondering what it was all about.

He said, 'Mr Wagner has been living under an assumed name since he came to Australia in 1919.'

It turned out that his real name was Carl Sturmer, one of the finest musicians of his time. He had given a recital in a provincial city in England and, while driving back to his home in Oxford with his wife, was involved in an accident that killed his wife, but left him unhurt. The only other two people who knew his identity were his bank manager and his sister. Carl had left all that he owned to me.

Some time in my late teens I had decided that the rest of my life would be spent with Kate, and I was pretty upset when she went off to be a nun. I couldn't make any sense of such a bright, happy and carefree girl being locked up in a convent. Even so, it was a great surprise when, in less than two years, she was back home.

I was delighted to see her again but she had changed, a lot. We were no longer close friends, as in the past. I don't know if she felt she was a failure. She wouldn't talk about her time away.

The following Saturday morning was hot and humid. Sam came in, 'Hey Fergie, the cave?' A question rather than a statement. It was some time since we had been near the cave. I found Kate there, floating inside the cave. She had been dead for hours.

I've never had another girlfriend. That was nearly seventy years ago, and I've never mentioned her to anyone until now.

Life went on. Our little dance band played almost every week, sometimes two or three times a week.

There were several big old mallee trees in one of the 'highland' paddocks and Dad said, 'They'd be of more use as fence posts'. That was the worst day's work I've ever done. You'd be surprised how tough mallee trees can grow. The first one came down okay. I must have been a bit careless with the second one because the axe glanced off the hard wood onto my right foot, through my boot and well into my foot.

I threw the axe as far as I could. Dad said later that I could have been a champion in the hammer throw.

I managed to walk home, at least to within yelling distance of the house, before I passed out. I've walked with a slight limp ever since, but it hasn't been any great handicap, and a stiff foot never affected my fiddling. And so, the band played on.

The majority of the families in the region, including us of course, were Presbyterian, mainly of Scottish descent.

'We should have our own church!' John McCain said. 'I'm near the middle of Masons. You can have a corner of my place if it's all right by the council.'

Another canny Scot said, 'It'll cost money.'

'We're part of the Town Parish,' said one of the leading ladies. 'And I'll be happy to run a Sunday School for some of the young heathens, including my own.'

Mr Jones said that there was the remains of an old quarry in his top paddock, and there were plenty of strong, young men about.

To cut a reasonably long story short, we built ourselves a neat little church, of which we were justifiably proud.

An enormous leap in entertainment brought in the 'Talkies' and I well remember that the first one I saw and heard was '42nd Street', one of the first musicals. Some critics considered the song 'Shuffle off to Buffalo', 'most unsuitable for children' in 1933, I think.

That year brought a lot of water from excessive rain in the high country a thousand miles away, and caused a fair bit of worry to people living in low-lying areas bordering the Murray. Any sections of the bank that looked a bit weak were strengthened by hammering corrugated iron into the earth on the river side of the embankment. This stopped the earth being washed away.

A roster was arranged of the men of Masons Flat to continually patrol the whole length of the bank, day and night, so warning could be given if any earth began to slip.

Some of the neighbouring swamps were soon under water, and at Masons it reached almost to the top of the banks. Then at last the water level began to drop. Dad regained the use of his truck. It had been standing ready with the keys in the ignition and holding a ton of galvanised iron, in case of emergency.

It wasn't until 1956, and I was on the other side of the world, that a flood covered all the reclaimed areas along the lower Murray.

Just like the Murray River, time keeps rolling on. Church service kept its fortnightly routine and our family were among the regular attendees. The Reverend Johnston said one day, 'You'd make a good lay preacher, Ian.'

'I've thought of it, Reverend, but I don't think I'd qualify.'

'Could you spare one night a week for a few months to come and see me?' he asked. That arrangement suited me, and after a while I found myself taking the Sunday School and giving a short service for any parents who wished to stay. Even so, my music was too dear to me to give up.

Dad was starting to weary of cows, and after talking it over with Mum, decided to sell and retire into town. The girls had learned dressmaking and knew that the woman in the drapery shop was thinking of retiring too.

'What will you do if we sell?' Dad asked me.

'Just what I've wanted to do for quite a while, take my violin to London,' I said. 'Then I'll find out if I'm as good as I think I am.'

I still had a bit of the money that Carl had left me, enough for a one-way ticket on a ship that also had a dance band.

I'd only been half alive since Kate died.

The day I disembarked at Portsmouth, war was declared. I remember the date – it was my nineteenth birthday.

I still had a bit of money in my pocket. By playing in the ship's dance band and giving a few recitals, I had made more than my fare had cost. The recitals were a dedication to Carl who taught me never to neglect what he had called 'real music'.

The day after landing, I found my way to a recruiting centre, quite aware that I slightly exaggerated my limp. The sergeant examining me barked, 'Take your boot off! Not that one, the other one. Do you have any qualifications?'

'I'm pretty good on the violin,' I said with a grin.

Instead of giving me a blast, he wrote a few words on a card and said, 'If you march a hundred yards, even wiv' your boots on, that foot'll fall to bits.' Handing me the card he said, 'If yer any good, they'll welcome yer.'

The card directed me to Army Entertainment. I stayed in England for the duration, and I travelled with a few well-known names.

Even wars eventually finish, and as far as wars go, I'd had it easy.

Afterwards, I travelled the length and breadth of the British Isles with the ghost of Kate. I eventually found myself in a village halfway up Scotland's west coast, where the fishing people risked their lives daily for their daily bread, and where the worst of the wind and waves were gentled by the Isle of Kerrera.

The tallest and largest building was the kirk, and I soon made myself known to the Reverend McKie, middle-aged, rotund and bouncy as a rubber ball. Oh, don't get the idea that all Scots are dour, most of these villagers had been affected by their good pastor.

'If you've nowhere to stay, there is a small room at the back of the house, about the size of yourself and your boots and bag. You are most welcome to stay.'

Apart from meals, and cups of tea between them, we sat and talked until midnight, by which time he knew my entire life history – except Kate.

He had also mapped out my future. He latched onto the fact that I had been a lay preacher. 'And I can teach you the rest, for I taught youngsters like you for fifteen years, until I was sick of the sight of them. You're no worse than the worst of them.'

Years later, I moved into his room where there was room for a desk and a bookcase, on top of which lay my fiddle, where it gathered dust.

God help me, the ghost of an Irish Catholic girl, never left me.

The rest of Uncle Ian's exercise books were full of his fifty years as pastor to his flock.

Kunz & Hanrahan Drainage Contractors

Good Money

Dad was a drainage contractor, or drainer, from the time he emigrated to Victoria from South Australia in 1950, until he retired in 1982. In the early days, trenches for stormwater and sewerage pipes were dug by hand and the earthenware pipes were cemented together. Sometime after the drainer had completed his work, the job was inspected by representatives of the Melbourne Metropolitan Board of Works. You might be able to infer Dad's opinion of draining, inspectors, weather and the MMBW.

Rain! You could always rely on the Melbourne weather. Sure, rely on it to do the wrong thing. Here it was, near the end of January, Monday morning, and the rain was coming down as though it would never stop.

The sky was lead-grey, with not the slightest change of shade in any direction.

'Humid at first, possibility of showers.' This shower had started eight hours ago. Marty and I had sent the whole gang home by nine o'clock. The work site was a sea of mud, except where the heaps of broken up basalt stuck up out of it.

I'd told him Thursday evening we had better ring Les for a couple of tip trucks and get the useless stuff out of the way, but he said there'd be more of it by the middle of next week and Les'd still move it all in a day.

Now, no-one in their right mind would try to get a jeep in off the road, let alone a twelve-yard tipper. I'd given up trying to figure in metres and metric tons, or whatever the blasted idiots who had never handled earth or rock or materials in their lives were trying to shove down our necks with their metric conversion. If you tried to prise their metric behinds from the swivel chairs behind the shiny two-square-metre desks, their milligram brains would cease to function.

Drainers have enough to worry about without trying to send themselves further around the bend by becoming metric converts.

Even the Board Inspectors were going further off their rockers with the strain of trying to think. If they had the power of thought, they'd never have been Board Inspectors, any more than Marty and I would have been drainers.

Well, I am a drainer anyway, but I doubt if my stubborn, bull-necked, bog-trotting, flat-footed Irish partner had ever seen a drainpipe until he came to Australia four years ago. Sure, he could work all right. So can a donkey, if it wants to, and like a donkey, Marty never had enough nous not to want to. Two years we'd been together, and now we had nearly as much as when we started.

'You must be going well, there's good money in draining.' Don't tell me, brother, all I ever had is in it and looks like staying there. Every time I rang the potteries a voice would say 'We've been expecting your cheque, Mr Kunz – incidentally, if you're pricing, remember an extra ten percent, as from the end of last month.' Always the end of last month, not next month, in case we ordered a couple extra and did them out of their inflated ten percent.

If they got a cheque from 'Mr Kunz', we'd have had the added problem of having to deal with an invisible bank manager.

'I'll see if Mr Grandison is in, Mr Kunz.'

'No, I'm sorry, Mr Kunz.' But, if Mr Grandison thought I had a dollar in my pocket, he'd have been at the door to meet me.

'But the accountant wondered if you would step into his office.' I'll step right on the accountant one day.

Things had gone really well last week. The gang had worked like Trojans – some of them right up to morning tea-break – and by Friday night, we had a nice long straight trench right across the estate. The backhoe operators knew their job, and were worth a good half of the exorbitant rates Les charged us. At least his machines and men were good and they moved some earth in a day. Les would have cried if he'd seen the way Leon got into the rock with the new hoe, and a yard of rock is still a yard of rock no matter how it comes out of the ground.

There's nothing wrong with working in greasy black clay when it's dry, even if it is stuffed with bluestone, and you have to expect it in this area.

Up until Friday, we'd gone well with Marty and Gino laying pipes. I was the boss – manager perhaps – of the team. that meant I mixed concrete, cleaned out the trench bottoms, formed up man-holes, wheeled barrows of screenings, got the lunches, took levels, fed material to Marty and Gino, argued with pottery reps, pacified Board Inspectors, made up wages, did most of the blasting, timbered up trenches, interpreted plans and bylaws, squared off with council engineers when back-hoes hooked into storm water drains, or the gas company when they hooked into a gas main, or the PMG when some phones went dead – and all this was on my easy days. Then, after knockoff, Marty would say 'You'll clean up and lock up, it's been dry and hot so I'll take Gino for a couple o' beers – he's done a moighty job on that nine-inch.'

'Kunz and Hanrahan – Drainage Contractors'. That's what it said on the sign on the door of the battered, galvanised iron shed that was storeroom, site office, changing room and lunch room. I had offered to change my name to O'Kunz when Marty said he'd never live it down working with a square-head, but then I said if I had to swallow my pride, so could he. We argued a lot, but never quite came to blows, which says plenty for my quiet, peaceful disposition, because if anyone could work for two years with the pig-headed, self-opinionated, ignorant clot that had never learned to keep his own temper, and not come to blows, he'd be close to being a saint.

Marty and I stayed at the site after the others had left, and were sitting in the tin shed, at what had once been a kitchen table, having a cup of tea and not feeling very cheerful as we listened to the rain drumming on the roof. I was studying the plan where a problem had cropped up – engineers were not infallible. Hanrahan was reading *The Sun*.

I said, 'They've made a blue of ten inches in the invert at the third manhole.'

Marty said, 'Sure, you should of rung Les on Thursd'y about gettin' the rock away, or didn't you remember to get the figures off old Dick?'

I looked up, 'You said, leave the rock and get the lot away in one go.'

'You'd need three trucks to move that in a day, even if you could get them in through the mud, so you could of had two in last week and one this week.'

Still calm and collected, I reminded him that he had said two trucks would do it.

'As well they could, if you'd had the sinse to move it while it was dry 'n all. Why do ye stubborn square-heads never like to raisin?' As though I never listen to his many and varied 'raisins'.

'It might pay us to put a few more soldiers in the deep end. Dick won't go down there now if we don't.' Soldiers are timbers standing upright in the trench and braced with toms to hold the sides up.

'Sure, I'd have done it Frid'y if I hadn't been layin' pipes ahll day, anyhow let old Dick test it from the top, he always does.'

'Only when Gino or I do the laying,' I told him.

'There's nothin' wrong with the way I lay.' He sounded as if I'd offended him, nothing was further from my mind. 'You should have taken that lump o' rock out loik I said, anyhow.'

'How's your crook wrist?' I asked.

'What crook wrist would that be now?' he wanted to know.

'Oh, I thought you couldn't pick up the hammer.'

'Sure, an' do you want me to do the whole job then?' His voice was rising.

'Of course not, Marty,' I said gently. 'I don't mind doing my share, and half yours.'

He slammed his great hand down on the table, and his mug of tea went all over his paper.

I passed him the billy of tea to calm him down a bit and said, 'Did you have enough tea or will I tip this on it too – you should read *The Age*, it holds more.'

Even that didn't pacify him. 'If I hadn't been talked into this partnership with yer Blarney, and put ahll me money into it, I'd knock yer block off and walk out on ye roit now. Yer nothin but a pain in the neck, a thorn in me soid, and its only me good nature'll kape me here and git ye out of the mess ye've got us both into.'

He got up angrily and started to put on his raincoat. 'Take the whisky with you', I offered.

'An' whoi?'

'You can hock it and get your money back out of the partnership.'

He didn't quite wreck the shed as he slammed the door – just as well, as I'd helped him put it up.

I put my own raincoat on and we sloshed through the mud to the deep end of the job. He lowered himself down into the greasy, slimy trench, and I started passing timber to him. By lunch time we'd made the dangerous section reasonably safe. I was wet and miserable and wishing I'd never seen him or the job. Marty was wet and whistling merry Irish airs and was as happy as if he was in his own native bog lands. The heavy timber was flicked into position, each tom whacked home one-handed with a hammer that I'd have to use in two hands, and I really had to gallop to keep him supplied with material.

'Sure, I've done a good job fer ye. Now I'll buy ye a beer and some lunch, even though ye owe me a couple already.' His kindness overwhelmed me and I met kindness with kindness.

'I'll buy the beer and lunch, it was your turn last week – it wasn't your fault you'd done all your money at the races and you had to use mine.'

'Jist as ye say, thin', said Hanrahan, determined for once not to argue.

On the way back to the shed I thought I'd check another section of the trench where the pipes were laid, and looking down, saw that a cover had been left off an inspection opening and there was a lump of clay in it.

'Sure, ye were last along here, ye should have seen to it.'

'You laid the pipes and should have put it on,' I explained mildly.

I climbed down the timber I had put there on Friday, and as I stepped onto the top tom it slipped with my weight. I kept on going down, knocking out more toms as I went. The wet, greasy clay near the top of the trench gave way, and the unsupported timber fell sideways along the trench, dislodging toms as it went. Then came a moment of sheer panic as I saw the side of the trench move in on me. The timbers on along one side were pushed over, snapping with the weight of the sodden earth. I was pushed onto my hands and knees into the trench bottom. Fortunately, the broken timbers bridged across me, or I'd have been crushed at once. As it was, I was in complete darkness, trapped by I didn't know how many tons of earth.

I'd been in a few situations when I'd thought I was scared, but the memory of the brain-searing panic that overwhelmed me then, still wakes me up screaming at night.

The suddenness, the weight of the slimy clay, the darkness and the near suffocation combined, and it was the pain in my fingers and the hoarseness in my throat that made me realise that I'd been yelling and trying to tear myself clear from the imprisoning timber and clay. Afterwards, when my brain began to function again, I remembered hoping that Marty couldn't hear my screams of terror at that moment.

Somehow, my brain did come back to some sort of sanity and I realised there was nothing I could do but wait and hope the pocket of air would last long enough to allow me to stay alive until Marty could return with help. Clay and timber was pressing into my back, and every now and then I could hear and feel it move. With every movement of the earth, black fear would flood my brain and, involuntarily, my fingers would start clutching at the clay. Then there was a long period of silence, and I hoped that the clay had stopped moving. I was cramped and light-headed, but trying to think. Air, I longed for it.

Hurry, Marty, you great, slow ox, I was saying to myself. Then I remembered why I'd gone down there. My right knee was being crushed against a six-inch diameter earthenware pipe full of beautiful clear, fresh air and somewhere, perhaps within inches, was the inspection opening clogged up with mud. I tried to move my right arm. My elbow was already digging painfully into my abdomen, but I managed to push my fingers into the clay and feel the smooth roundness of the pipe. I forced my fingers to move forward and soon felt the collar of the straight pipe on which I was kneeling. A few inches further should be the round top of the inspection opening, which was halfway between two manholes about a hundred feet apart.

Anxiety and panic gripped me for a few moments, and I forced myself to keep still for a while. I then started worming my hand towards the opening in the pipe.

Yes, there it is! My wrist was nearly breaking as I tried to force my hand into it. If I could push the clay down the pipe, air from the upper end of it should keep me going, provided the earth didn't squash me. The hard, sharp inner edge of the opening was cutting into the back of my fingers. But I could also feel the lump of clay sliding a fraction of an inch along the pipe. My head and chest felt as if they were bursting, but I kept pushing, and suddenly the clay slid along the inside of the pipe, and a draught of cool fresh air hit my face. I didn't know how beautiful air was until that moment, and I knew I had a reasonable chance of survival.

My hand hurt and it was trapped in the opening, but that was okay, now that I could breathe. I breathed as deeply as I could, and tried to figure out how long I'd been there. It seemed hours, but I knew it couldn't have been. Had Marty been able to get help? Was he back? My fingers were wet with the trickle of water running through the pipe, and I made a half-hearted attempt to get my hand out. So what if my fingers got wet.

Then I panicked again and tore at my hand. If the water wasn't getting past the lump of clay I'd pushed along the pipe it would fill up and cut off my air supply. There was still plenty of air coming through, and I didn't think it could seal off completely. I tried to convince myself that it couldn't

Movement in the timber pressing on my shoulder brought another wave of fear, but I realised I could feel a slow rhythmic vibration, steady and even – just about the speed of a man working with a shovel.

The relief of knowing that I was no longer alone gave me confidence, and from habit I started to condemn Marty for taking so long to get back with help. Maybe he hadn't even cared much whether he got back in time or not. He probably knew enough to realise I was probably beyond help and that there was no point in hurrying. Then I felt a solid thump of the shovel on the timber and a lessening of pressure against my aching shoulder.

I put all the strength I had left into my shoulder and the timber moved. A miniature avalanche of clay scattered around me. Daylight made me close my eyes and the rain-filled air was sweet beyond imagining. Someone was tearing at the timbers, and strong hands gripped my shoulders. The most beautiful sound I'd ever heard was a thick Irish brogue saying, 'God, man, are ye all right?'

I was stiff and sore and sick, my legs felt as though they were broken, and my back ached, but I was all right. I could never in all my life remember feeling more all right. The air was sweet, the rain was beautiful, and just to lie there in the soft wet clay, gazing up at the glory of the grey, leaden clouds that looked as though they'd never break, was the most joyous thing I'd ever known.

'Can ye get up, boy?' there was an unusual, breathless gasp in Marty's voice.

Then I looked at him, his great bare shoulders were wet with rain, grey with clay and sagging from complete exhaustion.

I dragged myself to a sitting position, looked at the mountain of wet glutinous mud that had buried me, at the two shovels with their handles broken off, and a third one still sticking in the earth.

'You did it on your own?'

'Sure, and who else would be troublin' to get ye out of the mess ye'd got yeself into an' all? Mind you, if it wasn't your turn to buy the beer and the lunch ...' He broke off and tossed Dick's bottle of scotch to me. We left a little bit for Dick and walked slowly and silently back to the shed. Marty lit the gas ring and put the billy on.

'The beer will keep and we're too late for lunch anyhow. Sure, and did you remember to put the top on the inspection opening while you were down there an' all?

Mates like Marty are hard to come by.

Let's Have a Beer

Jack Peckham was not all that bad, as far as I was concerned, but Marty never seemed to have a good word to say for him. Marty, of course, is the Irish half of Kunz & Hanrahan, Drainage Contractors, and one day I might tell you the long story of how I ever got tangled up with the great, overweight, pig-headed, bad tempered, unreasonable son of Erin. Then again, I may not.

'Peckham would knock back a job if Saint Patrick himself did it,' grizzled Marty when Jack hadn't been over-impressed with some of his work.

'Never saw a bishop yet could lay a drain,' says I. 'Besides, Saint Patrick was a Scotchman.'

'Sure, and what's a Scotsman but an Irishman that went to bed with the Poms?' he wanted to know. 'Even if he wasn't born in Ireland, at least he had enough sense to go there.'

'Does that make him brighter than you then?' I asked.

''Tis the best place on God's earth an' all.' There were storm clouds looming.

'And the worst leave it, and tell everyone how good it is.' I'm usually the peace maker, but I was a bit annoyed because Hanrahan always had the happy knack of antagonising Peckham, and life was hard enough without having to put up with upset Board Inspectors.

It had only been a minor fault in the drain, and if Marty hadn't started throwing out hints that Jack never knew the first thing about drains, and couldn't lay one if he tried, he'd have let us fix it there and then, cover it over, and no one would have been any the wiser, or any worse off either.

I made Marty the offer that next time we were in Peckham's territory, I'd lay the drains and he could do the work for a change, and there would be no trouble. Nothing seemed to please him and he snarled at me, 'The day I can't work you into the ground, I'll give the game away.'

'You've been working me into the ground the last couple of years,' I told him.

We were sitting in the front of the old one-tonner having a cup of tea from my flask. Marty had finished his, and was waiting for me to pass him the flask again. If he hadn't been in such a bad mood he'd have asked, so I let him wait.

'If Peckham was about twice his size, I'd knock his block off,' he growled.

'And that would be safe, because he'd still only be half your size,' I put in.

'And if I wasn't such an easy goin' fella, I'd have knocked yours off long since.' He was really upset.

'That and other reasons,' says I.

We went back to work, and in five minutes Marty was whistling away at some Irish tune, with all the melody and skill of a Kerry piper, and as usual, it was all up-hill keeping the materials up to him. We had the job looking the way it should have looked in the first place when we heard a car pull up in front of the house, and a minute later, Peckham was standing on the bank looking down at the big Irishman.

'Forget something, Jack?' I asked him.

He looked at me and winked, 'Just wondered if you knew how to fix it.'

For once, Hanrahan had the good sense not to look up, but I could see his taxi-door ears go red as he trowelled off the last of the joint. Jack started back to his car and I went with him.

'If you think water will run through it, instead of out of it, you can back-fill,' he said, loud enough for Marty to hear, and by the time I'd walked back to the job the Kerry pipes were skirling fit to set your feet tapping.

I had said to Jack, 'He's going to bury you down a trench one day.'

'Oh, Marty's okay, but when he starts to bounce he should expect someone to bounce back once in a while.'

We set about back-filling and I was pleased when Marty paused for a spell.

'You're still there then, I thought you had knocked off,' he said.

'You'd have been sitting in the shade long ago if you were left on your own,' I retorted.

He came back at me with, 'Only because I'd have finished sooner. I don't like working too hard in case you try to keep up and knock yourself out.' Then he asked, 'Is there any tea left?'

'I'll buy you a flask for your birthday,' and took him for a counter lunch instead.

The day was getting pretty warm, and we had put in a good solid morning's work. In these conditions it is not always a good idea to take an easily led Irishman for a counter lunch.

Just as luck would have it, Pat Phelan came into the bar, so I ordered three. He gave me the wink and said, 'Just had a test with Jack Peckham. He's an easy goin' lad for you now. He can pass a drain from the front gate, and him with his eyes shut.'

Marty came in like a hot north wind. 'No wonder you can't buy your own beer when you've just bought Peckham out,' he grumbled

'Sure, is that the only way you can get 'em passed?' asked Pat. 'Peckham said you'd learn to lay drains all in good time, but he reckoned you'd be better off takin' the old-age pension.' Then, to show he hadn't thrown away all his money, he bought the next round while he waited for his lunch.

We finished our whiting and chips and walked out to the car park together. Pat was working not far from where we were, so he said he would drop Marty back while I went and practised my juggling act at the bank. We were only a two-man team at this time, but still had to have something to take home if we wanted to survive the weekend.

I found there was yet another new teller behind the partition that kept money and drainers apart, and apparently the manager hadn't got back from lunch, so our starvation was averted for another week.

By the time I got to the job again, it was mid-afternoon, and nothing had been done since lunch, and there was no sign of Hanrahan.

'The black-hearted Phelan took him back to the pub,' I said to myself. My blood boiled.

There wasn't much use going looking for him, as he'd have lost the urge to work, so I grabbed my shovel and tried to work off my bad temper by getting the job cleaned up on my own, hoping I'd be finished before he turned up. Then he would have to go home broke, as well as bent, and he would get the rounds of the kitchen from his ever lovin' wife, and deserving every word of it. She was nearly as tall as he, if she stood on tiptoe on a kitchen chair, and he'd've reckoned that he had tangled with a shed full of wild cats, especially if she found out that he had hooked it from work all the afternoon.

I wasn't all that popular when I arrived home around five, going to town about alcoholic Irishmen who couldn't get back to work once they'd got the smell of a beer glass.

The phone rang before I had been inside ten minutes, and a soft, quiet voice said, 'Is it you then, Frank?' Kate Hanrahan, and I knew the next words would be, 'Where's Martin, do you know?' but I was wrong. Instead, she said, 'Martin said to ring you and say he reckoned Paddy was in no fit way to drive when they left the hotel, so he drove him home, and as there wasn't much back fillin' to do on your job, he went and filled in Paddy's job, knowin' ye wouldn't be doin' anything else for the rest of the day.' She gave a soft chuckle and went on. 'He sez the exercise would do you no harm, and you know how much trouble Phelan is in always. Then he'd be drivin' the car back to Phelan's, and would you pick him up there.'

That damn bog-trotter, everyone could get him to work except me. I should let him walk home, it's only four miles or so.

Well, I went to pick him up, and he's sitting in the Phelan's kitchen, drinking tea. Five-thirty on a hot Friday afternoon, and Hanrahan's drinking tea, and the Phelan kids waiting on him hand and foot.

There was no sign of Pat, so I did the right thing and accepted the cup of tea young Jenny poured for me, then sat yarning for a while. They are really great kids, it's a shame their father makes such a mess of himself, and then can't go back to work. He'd only had a couple of beers when I'd left after lunch. Now I knew why the wily Hanrahan was playing good neighbour, he'd dragged Pat back for one for the road, but it had no turning. Now he was trying to salve his conscience.

'Dad lying down?' I said to Jenny.

'Yes, Mr Kunz. He still doesn't feel too well. He'll be okay by morning.' Kids are more faithful than dogs. She would cover up for him, even though she knew that I knew. 'Mum's just gone to the shop. Should be back in a few minutes.'

Great, I didn't want my smarmy Irish mate to have to face her again that day, after the strife he's caused. I said we had better be going and could have cried when Jenny said, 'Thanks, Mr Hanrahan, Dad always says you're a good friend.'

I glared at Marty, hoping there was a pick handle in the back of the truck, and that I could get to it first. Marty was as cool as you please when we got outside, and I'm sure he'd have been satisfied not to mention the episode, so I said, 'What time did you leave the pub?'

He gave me a surprised look and said, 'When you did, we came out together.'

'How come Pat wasn't fit to drive?' I asked.

'Sure, didn't Kate tell you? Women, they talk all day and tell you nothing. When Pat was gettin' in the car, some idiot that shouldn't've been drivin' at all ran into his door as he was shuttin' it. Made a mess of his hand, so I ran Pat to the clinic. The doc gave him a needle to knock him out while he fixed it up, and told him to lie down for the afternoon.'

He looked at me a bit funny, and for a while I thought he was going to go looking for the pick handle.

'Only a mean-minded, suspicious, ingrate son of a square-headed Kraut would have thought we went back to the pub. I suppose you begrudge the bit of a hand I gave him, instead of coming back to give you a hand so you could knock off early. You couldn't give a damn for poor Pat, lyin' there on his back, with stitches in his hand, and fingers in plaster, and no money at the weekend for them lovely kids of his if he didn't get his job finished. For two pins I'd give you the back of me hand across that ugly puss, and if I'd had any sense at all I'd have teamed up with Phelan, instead of lowerin' the standards of the finest race on earth an' pairin' up with a whingin' Bock who couldn't get through an afternoon's work without the help of a real man, and then come round accusin' two honest, sober men of not bein' able to walk away from the pub to finish their week's work.' He hadn't stopped to take a breath.

Then he said, 'Have you got me wages?'

I handed him his share, not wanting to meet his eye.

'Ta,' he said. 'Come on, I'll buy you a beer.'

Mulvaney, of Course

I WOKE SUDDENLY IN THE dark of very early morning to a stabbing pain in the lower part of my rib cage, to hear a voice saying irritably, 'Mulvaney, of course.' Coming fully awake, I realised the voice was mine, and the stabbing pain was caused by my wife's elbow. It was no accident. I said, 'What do you mean – Mulvaney of course?' and she said, 'You said that when I asked, who is Mary.'

'What do you mean – who's Mary, then? And you can move your elbow, I'm awake.'

She took her elbow out of my ribs and I turned over to go to sleep again, well out of elbow reach.

'Well?' she said.

'Mmm? What? Well, what?' I asked grumpily.

'Who is Mary?' she said.

'Huh, Mary who?'

'Mulvaney, of course,' she snapped.

'You just said I said that. I don't know any Mary Mulvaney, so go to sleep. Anyway, what started this nonsense about Mary something?'

'Mulvaney. You were talking about her – to her, in fact. You said, "Oh Mary, the things we could do together".'

'You were dreaming. Good night.'

'It's morning, and you were talking to Mary.'

'Oh all right, next time you can come with me. I'll introduce you to her – Miss Mulvaney, meet my wife, Mrs Kunz.' I was getting sarcastic and just a bit disinterested in the conversation. Then I shot up into a sitting position and said, rather loudly, 'Did you say, Mary Mulvaney?'

'No, you did dear, now please go back to sleep.'

The situation had reversed and I had become the wide awake interrogator.

'But what do you know about Mary?'

'Mary who?' she mumbled sleepily.

'Mulvaney, of course.'

'Don't be cross, Dear. Get some sleep,' and she turned on her side, and honestly and genuinely started snoring. I know she wasn't pretending because she swears that she never snores – 'That tape is a fake,' she had said on a previous occasion, but that's another story that we won't go into right now.

I always sleep well, and never drink Scotch after midnight, but halfway through my second glass, the old clock in the lounge room struck four. I was sitting in the kitchen, convinced that I would never sleep again, at least not in the company I usually keep. That woman is a mind-reader and she snores. Besides, she is a witch. No, that was Mary Mulvaney, and I hadn't seen her for so long – in fact I hadn't thought of her for so many years that I couldn't remember if I had ever thought of her at all.

Apart from that, I didn't believe in witches, and they don't look like Mary. You know the colour of straw bleached in the hot summer sun? That was Mary's hair. And the winter sky after a frosty morning, way out in the wheat country up around the Port Buckley district? Her eyes were that sort of blue, with a sparkle of sunshine, and so alive. And have you ever stood back on a hill and looked at the beach? The sand isn't exactly creamy, nor as dark as honey, but looks so smooth and warm – her skin.

Oh blast! I tossed down the rest of my drink, made my usual mental act of acknowledgement to the wisdom of the Scots and went to bed.

The next thing I knew, the alarm clock was telling me the time had come to get up and go to work. I'm a successful contractor. That means I don't owe much more than last month's accounts for materials, which I should be able to settle with next month's cheques, if they arrive, and providing there is work for me to do. There usually is.

I was doing a small job behind a house in an inner suburb. At lunchtime, I came out to the street to see if I had a ticket for parking too long in the one spot. There was a chap parked behind me in a car with South Australian number plates. We passed the time of day – I have a compulsion to say good-day to South Australians – and I admitted that I had defected from over the border. 'And raised the overall standards of both states,' he said.

I was still trying to work that one out when he said, 'Port Buckley? Mary Mulvaney was my father's housekeeper for years – she's a witch.'

I didn't recall mentioning Port Buckley. I guess I had a sillier than usual look on my face and stared at him as though I hadn't seen him before. He was staring back at me reflecting my own look of blank surprise.

He went red and said, 'What a damned silly thing to say.'

I would have agreed with him, only he remembered an urgent appointment and took off like a low flying jet, as if a witch was after him.

I was a little distracted as I started the ute to go looking for some lunch, wondering if I had really heard what the man said, or if I was still dreaming. It was eight hours since I'd had anything stronger than tea.

How many people in their fifties can remember exactly what someone looked like when they were six? I mean when the people in their fifties were six. I was only about six or seven when I had last seen Mary Mulvaney. She was in her early twenties, and I knew exactly what she looked like. Maybe I remember because she looked like that. Well, I mean she was something to remember, wasn't she? If any of the rest of her family had wanted to be witches they'd have had it made, but not Mary. Oh, no.

They lived in the big old limestone house with the green painted iron roof. It was on the hill just up from the town centre. From the front verandah you could see the beach, and the jetty that always looked too long for the rest of the town. It reminded me of a daddy-long-legs testing the bath water with an extended toe. There was a sign on their front gate that introduced the intrepid visitor to the Misses Mulvaney – Piano Lessons, Singing and Elocution, and Dress Making. At social functions, Miss Monica played the piano for dancing, or accompanied Miss Mavis as she sang 'Bless This House' in her fine contralto, while Miss Maud's artistry was evident in the smartness of the frocks worn by the very best dressed local ladies.

The three sisters were very much alike in looks and manners, 'austere' is the word that most readily comes to mind. Queen Victoria would have approved of them in every way. I thought they were witches and approached their house in fear and trembling whenever I went there in the company of my older sisters, who were learning the piano from Miss M, whichever one was the pianist. It's so long ago, I'm not too sure now.

Even on a hot day, I'd feel shivery as I sat alone in the gloomy front room while my sisters were whisked off for their lessons. Anyway, the three elder Misses Mulvaney could have played the cauldron scene of Macbeth without make-up or rehearsal.

Mary was never there, as she ran a tearoom in the High Street, flirting with the men, and laughing with their wives as she whispered all the latest gossip into their ever ready ears. Everyone loved Mary, and she in turn loved everyone, and one by one she gave all the young men the brush off, laughing in their faces with her blue eyes dancing, and her long, soft hair – with its little blue bow at the nape of her neck – swinging almost to her waist. She was too plump to be a model, but only just too plump, and if the women said she shouldn't wear her skirts so short, the men would say, 'But she's only a girl.' And she wasn't. Besides, they were not all that short, nobody wore short skirts in those days.

All right, I was only six, and I don't know why I remember her so well, but suddenly I do. After not even thinking about her for forty-odd years. No witch ever looked like that.

Whenever I went into the cafe with my parents, she'd be there at the table as soon as we were seated, with the birds of spring singing in her voice as she chatted to us. I knew what she would do, and I'd wish she wouldn't because it embarrassed me so much, but then I'd be afraid she wouldn't. As she walked behind my chair she'd pause a moment, put her hands lightly on my shoulders so they touched my reddening neck, then with a laugh that was almost a gurgle she'd say, 'And how is my Francie with the pretty curls.' Everyone else called me

Frank. Dad would be grinning at me and Mum wouldn't. However, next time I'd have my hair wet and brushed down flat before I left home. By lunchtime, it would be dried in the breeze, each springy wave neatly in place. Now, when I want them, they've gone.

It must have been some time in the summer, maybe January, because one of the last of the sailing ships which used to take the wheat, was being loaded at the jetty. I was more interested in the activity wharfside than I was in having afternoon tea with my parents. Mum said, 'Don't go down along the jetty though, you'll be in the way of the men, and it's not safe.'

I don't really remember any of the ensuing events. But what happened never made much sense, then or now, and until my beloved's elbow started me thinking about Mary Mulvaney, I'd forgotten it completely, even though my mother had spoken frequently about it for some time afterwards.

The tearoom was a hundred yards or so from the beach, and I was sitting on one of the playground swings. After a few minutes, I conveniently forgot to stay put, and wandered down onto the jetty, being careful not to go too far or cause any obstruction to the men. I was no longer in view of the tearoom.

When Mary came along to the table she said, 'Mrs Kunz, where is my Francie?' She was told that I was at the beach watching the ship being loaded. Mary said, 'Tell him how sad I am that he would rather watch the ship than see me.' She winked at Dad, and I don't think for a moment that he would have preferred watching the scruffy little wheat boat.

When she came back with the tea and cakes, she was chatting away with them as she approached the table. She stopped in mid-sentence, the tray poised a few inches above the table. Her face suddenly went white as she said quite clearly, but almost in a whisper, 'My

Francie!' Then the tray crashed down, scattering its contents across the table, and she had turned and was out the door and running towards the jetty.

My parents followed her out. She had reached the shore end of the jetty by the time they had gained the street. It probably took them only a second to realise that I was no longer on the swing and was nowhere in sight, but hadn't had time to gather their scattered thoughts to consider that anything might have happened to me.

There was no one on the jetty nearer than the section that ran at right angles at the end of it. Mary was still running at top speed and was halfway along, where part of the safety railing was missing. Without slackening, she was over the side and she disappeared below the surface.

Dad reached the spot well ahead of Mum, and he said it seemed ages before Mary surfaced, though it must have only been a few seconds. Had it been longer I wouldn't have still been alive. As it was, I began to splutter into consciousness almost as soon as she dragged me into one of the several skiffs moored alongside the jetty. Dad said he could hear her sobbing and talking at the same time, but couldn't make out what she was saying. Then she scrambled up onto the jetty, and without a backward glance at me lying coughing and spluttering in the boat, she ran back to the now deserted tearoom. She served no more teas that day, nor would she come to the door when Mum went to see if she was all right.

I never knew what she meant when in the boat she had sobbed, 'Oh Francie, thank God. I always know where you are – the things we could do together.' Mum said I must have imagined it, and Dad said it was lucky she acted so fast when she saw me go over. Then they would look at each other in that way parents have when they think they are putting something over on their kids. No one thought to mention the fact that I was out of sight of the tearoom when the rail I was swinging on had broken.

Mary married some character soon after and I haven't seen her since. It's funny that that bloke had called her 'Mary Mulvaney' instead of Mrs Whoever-she-is.

I do remember walking in on a conversation between my parents just as Dad said, 'I've never seen any one less like a witch, what damn rot.'

'Who's a witch, Mum?' I asked.

'Whatever are you talking about, no one said anything about witches.'

I don't know why I should wake up nearly half a century later, in the small hours of the morning talking about Mary Mulvaney, but I have a bruise on my ribs to prove that I did.

Weekend

MARGARET AND HELEN HAD spent the day talking. Old times, good times. Young friends who had grown even firmer friends over more years than they cared to admit. They had laughed a lot, cried a little and enjoyed themselves immensely. Helen had gone into her tiny kitchen to make coffee, leaving Margaret watching the late news. 'A middle-aged man and a young woman were killed this evening when their station wagon ran off the road and struck a tree …' As the camera panned across the scene of the accident, it took in the wrecked car, resting momentarily on the rear number plate, LBH-196. Still talking, Helen returned to the lounge room carrying the tray of coffee and biscuits. 'Marg, I've even got some of those cream biscuits you used to eat by the pack.'

Margaret was sitting upright, gripping the arms of her chair, white-faced and rigid with shock. 'It's our car – it's our car – and a woman,' she muttered over and over.

By eight o'clock, I had eaten my greasy fish and chips while my favourite Beethoven had entertained me on the stereo – an unheard of luxury. The TV remained cold and silent in the corner. I burned my tea dishes in the briquette heater and relaxed with the last of the medicinal brandy. I had never had it so good – this was living.

I sat back with my heels higher than my head, heater on, book open on my chest, at peace with the world, and began to wonder what dread capers Mike would get up to, what my dearly beloved was saying about me, hoping she wasn't missing me too much, and who was keeping their eye on Chris to see she wasn't straying from the paths of righteousness. For a moment of weakness and panic I asked why families couldn't stay put and spend weekends together in their own homes, instead of forever splitting asunder and wandering all over the globe without the steadying influence of parents, so necessary to them all.

Come to think of it, I had got a nasty look from my better half when her old school chum had arrived to collect her, all because I said, 'Wow – you were in Marg's class at school?'

How was I to know she was going to look like that? Not that I'm complaining about the way Margaret looks, but in all fairness, if she came in looking blue-eyed and corn silky, wearing a fortnight's wages that just matched her eyes and didn't anywhere reach her knees, I'd say she was mutton dressed up as lamb. Well, that's how the girlfriend looked, and no hint of mutton, so the most obvious thing to say was, 'Wow'.

Now the average, honest to goodness, run of the mill drainer would have hunted up some of his old cronies and had, if not a lost weekend, at least one that would have been damned hard to find afterwards, but I'm a misfit that has strayed so far from the straight and narrow that I've acquired a taste for Debussy and books, rather than betting and beer. I've even tried my hand at writing a few yarns and some poetry – jingly sort of stuff mostly, but a bit of corny soul stuff as well. It keeps me off the street, but it's just as well I can lay drains.

As usual, I woke early and had the morning paper for breakfast Then growled because it was too wet to mow the lawn. I tossed a change of clothes into the station wagon, together with some writing material, and headed away from the big smoke to the peace and quiet of the wide-open spaces. I knew that, in the right atmosphere, I could bring into the world its long awaited literary masterpiece, complete with a blue-eyed and corn-silky heroine.

Footloose and fancy-free, I had a quiet cruise up the rain-polished highway, enjoying the greens and greys, pleased that I wasn't working out in persistent drizzle. As I drove, I tried to nut out some sort of a beginning for a short story. After a while, I turned down a gravel road and parked alongside a bend of the Goulburn River, had some coffee from my thermos and began to write.

I'm a slow writer, and thoughts don't come with any great rush either, but I soon lost track of time and my surroundings as the fruits of my great intellect transferred themselves to paper, almost in spite of myself. I tell myself, and everyone else, that I write only because it is completely relaxing and doesn't burn up physical energy. I refuse to admit that I'd give anything to have my great works published. 'Francis Kunz, well-known author and poet'. Oh well, it's not everyone that can lay drains.

Some time after midday, I realised that I had filled quite a number of pages with scrawl and also that I was about to have company. A bedraggled looking individual was approaching the car. At first, I wasn't sure if it was male or female. Blue jeans, khaki jacket and a peaked denim cap, from under which poked dark, collar-length hair. By the time it had reached the car, I decided that it was feminine and wondered what she was doing here alone, walking on a day that wasn't made for walking. She was around twenty, I guessed.

As she reached the car, I wound down the window and said, 'Not much of a day for bush walking.'

'Aw – no – well, my car stopped, y'know, and won't start. I sort of don't know about cars and wonder if you can help me somehow.'

I'm not my idea of a knight in shining armour and I must say she was not my idea of the fair maidens in distress that I had dreamed up from time to time.

'I feel awful asking for help, but there's no one else around and – well – what can I do?'

I didn't know what she could do, so I asked her where her car was and was told, 'Just around the corner, you could see it if it wasn't for the trees. It's a wonder you didn't hear it, or were you sleeping?'

Before I could answer she had spotted the sheets of scribble – I'm a bit self-conscious about calling it a manuscript.

'Gee, you must like letter writing, must've taken you hours to write all that, wouldn't it be quicker to ring up – or aren't you talking?' She was one of those types who can keep a monologue going, without waiting for answers or even realising that she was asking questions.

'Well ya must be hard up for something to do to sit around writing all day, or are ya writing ya life story? Wouldn't be too exciting if all ya do is sit under a tree by y'self, it's not my idea of a weekend, or are ya some sort of kook or something? Aw, gee, I'm not very nice to ya, and I only meant to ask ya to help me, not to stand here shooting off at ya, and it's none of my business how ya spend ya weekends, just wouldn't do me that's all – do ya reckon ya could help me?'

I was in no hurry to invite her into the car, and was somewhat relieved when she said, 'Look, I'm wet and all messed up and it's not raining now hardly at all, and it'll only take a minute to walk, so can't ya at least have a look, it mightn't be much and I wouldn't know, ya know?'

Reluctantly, I got out of the car. She had already set off towards her car, talking as she went, telling me how decent I was to lend a hand, that she needn't have said I was a kook, and maybe ya could have a good time sitting around writing letters by yerself or whatever, but that she'd never tried it and didn't think she would. Then she stopped a dozen or so paces ahead of me, turned and said, 'Sucker!'

The sun set, the stars flashed out and darkness fell, suddenly and painfully.

After a quiet rest of unknown period, daylight returned, and with it a screaming, throbbing pain behind my right ear. For a moment I wondered why my beloved had taken all the blankets and what I had done to merit such treatment. Then, some memory of what had happened seeped into my aching head, and I knew the meaning of the word 'sucker'. I felt unwell, which is not pleasant when one has suddenly become a pedestrian – even if one could get up and walk.

My manuscript had been placed in a neat, very thin, little pile where my car had been when I had last seen it. She had even used a smooth, round stone for a paperweight; and I bet she never stopped talking all the while.

Apart from the painful swelling behind my ear, the neon lights inside my head, the fact that I couldn't focus too well, and the added discomfort that I had discarded everything I'd had to eat or drink that morning, I was, to coin a phrase, as well as could be expected under the circumstances.

It was a long way home and my wallet was in my jacket pocket in the car. There were no publishers around to whom I could offer my sodden manuscript. I was wet. I struggled to my feet and soon came up with the idea that my best plan was to sit down again before I fell down. I sat, leaning back on the trunk of the tree, behind which the young lady's travelling companion had been waiting while she went through her act. When the clouds thinned enough for me to locate the sun, I estimated that it was mid-afternoon and that I had been out of it for well over an hour.

After due consideration, I figured that there was nothing to be gained by sitting there for the rest of the day. I felt miserable and cold, and soon discovered that standing was no longer impossible, and that my legs were still usable, even though my head was not of much value. Fortunately, I had no pressing engagements and my family wouldn't be worried about me. That is the meaning of lonely.

A quarter of an hour later, I found that the sucker bait had at least been telling some truth. Also, I knew enough about cars to diagnose the trouble with hers. It was nose down in the river after having skidded off the road and gone down the river bank for a drink. I also knew how to rectify the problem, but unfortunately, I had no tow truck with me at the moment.

I walked on, sadly and slowly, wishing I had never developed a liking for quiet roads on wet days. It was only a couple of hour's hike back to the highway, and fortunately, some good-hearted truck drivers are not all that fussy about the look of the hitchhikers they pick up. This particular Samaritan was not at all perturbed at going quite some way out of his normal route to make sure I got home without any further misadventure, and while I cooked bacon and eggs, he went off to the pub to get some brandy to replace what I had knocked off last night.

I was feeling pretty good by the time he finally left, and after a long hot shower, I settled down to watch the late news.

Then I dialled Helen's number.

The Rest of the Stories

The Rock

H E NEVER KNEW HOW the rock had got there, whether it was the result of some geological freak, or if it had been placed there by human hands. The great slab was the same material as the rock formation on the beach, at the foot of the rugged cliffs that made the little headland. The first time Jim Cronin saw it was when he'd walked out to look across the sea. It was there, smooth and flat, its grey surface warm in the afternoon sun. He had sat there with his thoughts thousands of miles across the ocean, and his heart was warm with the love he had for the girl who would soon come to him.

'As soon as I have a little money put by, Darlin'.'

And she said, 'I'll be impatient for you, Jim.'

Then the little boat had taken him across the sea to England where he was alone and sad in the noise and greyness of London. The huge city frightened him, so he was glad when the ship was far from the sight of land. His heart was peaceful, though lonely, and he looked forward to his arrival in Australia, where he'd work and wait.

Everyone was talking of towns in Australia being paved with gold. But, when he arrived at the diggings, the streets of mud depressed him, and the noise of the miners, as they spent their hard-earned money, brought back the fear and loneliness that had haunted him in London. He had lived in sight of the sea all his life, and the clean sea air called to him. There were jobs available at the diggings for honest working men who were not under the spell of the desire for gold. He stayed there for a year. Then he heard of a township on the coast, where the soil was rich and the sea was filled with fish ready for the catching.

On the day of his arrival he had walked out along the cliffs. The rolling countryside was green underneath the blue and white of the sky. His heart was at peace, for he knew he was finally home, and it was here he would work and wait.

His year's savings would bring Norah to him. And there was enough left to secure the small area of land that surrounded him as he sat and dreamed: The rock was a firm foundation. Its solidity would be always there. The world would age and change around it, but like eternity, the rock was immune from change.

Jim was soon building a cottage. Smooth slabs of local stone were laid for the foundations and the floors. The walls were built firm and strong, in the manner of the home of his youth. The windows and door looked across the sea. A few yards from the cottage door was the rock where Jim would sit of an evening. There was peace about him and his simple home. He was alone, but never lonely.

When her ship arrived, and when he looked again into the blue-grey eyes, so much like the sea that had brought her to him, he knew that he would never be alone again. In the long moment that he held her to him, and when the softness of her hair was against his cheek, he thought their love was as warm and steadfast as the rock.

They were married in the early morning cold of late winter, at the church in the heart of a village that was already growing into a town.

He brought her home in sunshine. Before he carried her across the threshold of the cottage, they sat together on the great smooth stone. The blue and green of the ocean in front of them seemed to be one with the blue sky and the green fields. They sat close, as young lovers will, their heads leaning to each other, their lives joined for as long as the rock on which they sat would last. They and the cottage built firm by the strength of his hands, became one, and peace surrounded them.

Jim had adopted a ritual of spending a few moments where the rock overlooked the sea, where he gave thanks for all that was theirs, before turning to the cottage. She would be waiting there for him, sometimes seated with her back to the sea so she would see him as he came along the cliff tops, sometimes looking out across the water and she would feel the touch of his hand on her shoulder before she would hear the sound of his footsteps over the noise of the waves. Then they would sit close for a while, for they were still lovers.

'Sure, I believe you love that slab of rock more than me,' she would say, her eyes mocking him. 'I never know if you'll kiss it or me first.'

'Norah, darlin,' the strength of it is like the strength of our love.' And he would hold her, and she knew it was not the rock at all that he loved more.

On a Sunday, with the fat little pony between the shafts of the light cart, 'dog cart' he always called it, they'd travel the two or three miles to Church and yarn with the neighbours for an hour, or maybe more. Their happiness would show in the laughter-filled conversation outside the little church, until Father would say, 'Be off with you now. Your neighbours will have no character left at all.' The mixture of horse-drawn vehicles would disperse towards their various destinations, and pedestrian groups to their homes in the township.

Perhaps a neighbouring family would accompany Jim and Norah home, or maybe the Cronins would take lunch with the O'Briens, who grew potatoes and onions and kept a few cows. Paddy and Jane O'Brien were their closest neighbours – 'closest' is a better word than 'nearest'. After the four lively O'Brien children and their parents had spent a Sunday lunch at the cottage, the place would seem too quiet for a while.

'Sure, we have so much, Norah darlin', is it right we should be askin' for more?' Jim would say, and whether they asked or not, no more came and they accepted what they could not change.

The little plot of land was not enough to support them, so Jim worked where he could for the farmers and the fishermen. They led a simple, quiet life together. Their needs were few.

Then one day after Mass, O'Brien said to Jim, 'Joe Carlin is sellin' his boat and buying a farm. 'Tis a fine small boat, and sturdy, and you know the sea and boats and all.'

'And you're not one to turn down a Sunday afternoon on the water when the weather's good and the snapper bitin',' Jim told him.

The two men laughed, and their wives said what a fine thing it would be to have a few quiet hours without them, so they could talk instead of having to listen.

So, the boat was closely looked over and her sturdiness was evident in every beam and plank of her and the next few years showed the sea yielding up a living for the Cronins, as long as they were content to live quietly and keep their vegetables growing and the poultry laying.

Norah loved the sea and the boat and, whenever young O'Brien was not available to crew the boat, or if he wanted to spend the day and his hard-earned wages with one or another of his pretty admirers, she would lend a hand with the crayfish pots and the nets. At home afterwards, she would be the warmth and peace that is the lot of two contented people. They would sit on the great rectangle of rock, close together, as if they were young lovers still, and say a prayer of thanksgiving together for all that was theirs.

'Sure, and a girl isn't safe to be out alone with you, Jim Cronin.' she would tell him, laughing.

'Any girl except you is, and you know it.'

He was still tall and straight, with the strength of a man who worked hard. She was slim, with her brown hair soft against his cheek as they stood together looking across the water. It was as though their lives had taken on the strength and solidity of the rock and the brightness of the water in the setting sun.

The years passed quickly, peacefully. If someone had said 'Is it ten years or more?' they would be hard put to be sure whether it might be twelve or fifteen.

'It was five years when the thatch caught fire, and you burnt your hands tearin' it down.'

'And it was two years – or three? – after that when I took the iron off because the house looked sad and ugly under it.'

'I know it's seven, no perhaps only six, since you did that, and wasn't that the year before you bought the boat?'

Their milestones were events that they had shared, rather than dates on the calendar, but they always knew when it was Sunday. On the afternoons when it was fine, and some that were not, just for a change, Jim would fish with a rod instead of a net and yarn with O'Brien; not caring whether they caught fish or not. Now and then they'd talk Father into joining them, knowing full well that if he had mentioned anything about 'casting nets into the deep' during his sermon, that he'd be with them anyway.

Even after a day with them he'd pause by the rock and Father would say, 'Sure, you keep your money bag under that rock,' and after giving it a kick, 'I'd repair the church roof if I could move it,' and he'd pretend to try to move the immovable from the non-existent wealth.

If the weather was warm, they would quite likely sit there for a while and give different theories as to how the slab came to be there, so far above its fellow rocks. Then the yarns they'd tell about previous fishing trips, and ones that got away, would be beyond believing, while Father ruined the fresh sea air with thick clouds of tobacco smoke.

At the accepted hour, Norah would announce that the tea would be cold in the cup if they didn't stir themselves, and they'd want to know why she had taken so long about it, and they dyin' o' thirst.

Then they'd turn to the cottage which, under its mellow slates, no longer looked sad and ugly. Amid laughter, Jim would find a bottle all the way from old Ireland and wonder out loud who had been at it and all.

Jim knew all the moods of the sea, and could tell by the swell when strong winds would come howling across it from a thousand miles away. That morning, while the air was cool and calm, he looked out at the long, slow movement of the water.

'We are in for a whale of a storm by evenin', girl,' He told Norah, and when young O'Brien came, they brought in the lobster pots. "Tis all the fishin' we'll do today.' They were back long before midday.

The wind had begun to rise, and within a couple of hours it was beating at the door and windows with a strength greater than the Cronins had ever experienced.

The swell of the sea had been transformed into mountains of water.

The ground around the rock was wet with spray as the breakers thundered against the cliffs. Years ago, Jim had made shutters to cover the windows, in case of severe winds, and today, for the first time, he fastened them in position, so that now, the only daylight in the house was that which came into the small kitchen at the rear, away from the fury of the storm.

He stood in the lee of the house, looking across the storm-lashed water. He saw one of the fishing boats from the township being driven towards the shore and feared for its safety. He went quickly through the back door; it was impossible to use the front one. 'Norah, there's one of the boats not in yet, and it's only a miracle that it's still afloat, no one in his right mind would have gone out on such a day. He'll most likely run on the beach halfway to town, he'll never make it around the point. I'll go out along the beach. He'll maybe need a hand, if he's lucky enough to make landfall.'

He was getting into his waterproofs as he spoke. 'Be careful, dear, and I'll have something hot for ye when you get back.'

Then he was striding quickly away, she with a prayer for him, and he with one for the boat and its crew. He reckoned that the craft would beach halfway along the curve of the coastline, where sandhills took the place of cliffs, a mile or so from the cottage. He broke into a run so as to be there when it struck. Norah put on her coat and went out to watch from the clifftop. She couldn't stay inside while Jim was out there in the wild of the gale.

It was difficult to stand, but as she reached the rock, she was in time to see the boat carried on a mountainous wave, as if it were a bit of driftwood, right up onto the slope of the sand dune, where it was left grounded.

Jim was still running and stumbling along the dunes. She could see that the two fishermen had leapt ashore by the time he reached them. It was dusk by now. She realised they would make the boat safe against the chance of another giant wave lifting it off the sand dune before they returned to the cottage.

She turned towards the sea with a prayer of thanksgiving, and at that moment a mountain of water broke with the sound of thunder against the low headland, and with such fury that a solid volume of water rose like a wall in front of her.

She turned to run, but too late. The water bore down on her and flung her against the rock.

It was almost dark when Jim and the fishermen arrived at the cottage. Jim wondered that the lamps had not been lit. He took the men into the warmth and peace of the kitchen and called to Norah. She was not in the house, and he turned again into the gale. He found her beside the rock. The grief that flooded his heart was one with the fury of the storm that had taken her from him. When the fury had passed, and the wind had spent its power, the joy and love he had known had gone with it. His eyes reflected his hopelessness. His heart broke with the blackness of his despair.

She was buried on the headland in front of the home she had made so happy for him, and the rock became her headstone.

Then, when Father and his friends and neighbours were gone, he knelt alone on the cold, grey smoothness of the rock.

He was reminded of the solidity of the rock. Peace came again. True love, too, is eternal. He only had to wait, just as he had so many years ago. His love would keep him going until the rock would become his headstone too.

The years passed, and nights were quiet. Jim spent more time at the rock on the headland, reliving the years they'd had together.

That summer had been hot and he couldn't remember the countryside being so dry in over fifty years.

All that day, the clouds had been building up around to the northwest until, in the late afternoon, they had obscured the sun, giving some relief from the glaring heat.

The evening was breathless. Jim felt old and tired, as though the humidity was pressing in on him and squeezing what remained of life from him.

He walked slowly to the rock that had become a shrine. It was now overshadowed by a huge flowering gum. The tree was sturdy, but twisted and bent, as it leaned away from the prevailing winds. The vivid crimson of its blossoms was the only relieving colour on the sunburnt land.

A light northerly was blowing, bringing with it the heat of hundreds of miles of thirsty plains. There was no coolness from the sea that lay calm and dark under the gathering thunder clouds.

The occasional flash of lightning, followed after a long interval by the rumble of thunder, gave evidence of an approaching storm and added to the oppressiveness of the atmosphere.

As the light faded, the lightning increased in brilliance, until the thunder cracked and roared in accord with the flash.

Jim had not felt like eating, but had made a cup of tea. The weakness he had felt before had been replaced by a sudden pain across his shoulders and chest. It was difficult for him to breathe.

He felt dizzy when he got to his feet and walked slowly, shuffling a little, towards the rock. When only a few feet from it, a searing flash of white lit the whole headland, and the thunderbolt seemed to explode on the cottage roof, scattering slates like shrapnel. The tinder-dry roof timbers burst into flames. The lone tree, showing crimson in the whiteness of the flash, was shattered as the fireball struck and the eternal, never-changing rock split with a deafening crack as of cannon fire.

Early the next morning, young O'Brien, his hair now grey with mounting years, called in to the cottage. The air was clean and cool after the night's heavy rain, and the breeze across the sparkling water was fresh on his face. He felt a shock of fear for his old friend when he saw the ruin the storm had caused. Then he saw Jim by the rock, a hand on either side of the crack that sliced clear through it.

The cheek resting on the cool, smooth surface was cold. Peace and contentment was on his face. He had found love that would outlive the changing rocks and the crumbling foundations of the world.

Dark

H E COULDN'T REMEMBER A time when to be alone in the dark was anything but a period of terror, and he could never quite remember why. Some event must have taken place in his early childhood, or perhaps one of his many nightmares triggered off something in his sub-conscious to bring on the fear.

The long, rain-filled winter nights in the country, far away from the comforting glow of street lights, had been the worst.

The farm was in the rolling country along the foothills. The looming ranges to the north and east seemed to crowd in on him, as though they had some animate life of their own. The blackness of night was unrelieved by star or moon. The sighing of the wind in the trees near the house, and the snare drum sound of the rain on the iron roof, and all the world was black.

No one ever considered him odd in any way, perhaps a bit quiet, but not dull or shy. At school, he was bright enough and always ready to take part in whatever sport or fun was going on. If he spent the greater part of the weekend alone, because there were no boys of his age group living near, it didn't seem to worry him. Sometimes, he would ride his bike to the Simpson place and spend the day with Toby, doing exactly what he would have if he'd stayed at home.

They might loiter around the farm sheds, just yarning, or put up a rabbit or two along the creek. Maybe Toby would know the whereabouts of a rosella's nest with young ones ready for kidnapping.

The days were easy, carefree and untroubled, and the quiet moonlit nights were ever a fascination to him, with their soft bush sounds in the rustling trees as they stirred sleepily in the mild north breeze that drifted, rather than blew, across the river flats and lifted gently up the slopes. It was good to be out of doors on summer evenings, or in the crisp coldn of the early winter frosts. Kids don't mind the cold if they can move around in the open air, especially if the night is light enough for the plume of smoke from the living room chimney to be seen, and to know that the welcoming warmth and brightness of the house was waiting.

He never thought of darkness while there was light. So, as long as there were enough stars to let him to see the oblong of the bedroom window as he lay facing it, the nights were peaceful.

However, there were the nights, black with cloud, with no comforting chink of light under the door after his parents had gone to bed. He would wake when night was the darkest, and it was the darkness that woke him, rolling in on him from all sides, suffocating, alive in its blackness, the terror of its invisible motion folding over itself, twisting, tenuous, writhing, tangling, choking.

He would pull the covers over his head and bite into the pillow to keep from screaming as the dark folded him in. He could even hear the dark as it moaned in the trees and beat on the roof to drip, drip, drip in the downpipes. He could feel it as it crushed against the house, against the blankets and against his head. Inside his head, the pain of it pressing on his brain would make him cry out in agony, and he'd lie panting and gasping, hoping no one had heard him. How he longed to reach out and turn on his bedside lamp, but the dark held him captive, his arms were helpless in its suffocating grip, just as it held his mind motionless, and empty of all else but the black terror of fear and despair. Even the longing he had for daybreak was gone in the overwhelming torture of the dark.

Then the all-powerful blackness would overcome the agony, there was nothing at all. Then his eyes would open to the soft light of dawn. He'd lie warm and comfortable, listening to the gentle rain.

Fully awake, his mind would go searching through the night, trying to remember if he had dreamed, or if he had been awake. The terror was only half remembered, the agony forgotten. Mum would be calling him to breakfast, or he'd be late for school.

'Do you feel all right, dear?' asked Mum. 'You look a bit pale.'

'Gee, I'm hungry. I suppose a fella can look a bit pale when he's starving.'

'Are you sure you slept well? I thought I heard you call out once, but you might have been dreaming,' his mother said, as she gave him his breakfast.

'I go to bed to sleep, not to dream,' he replied. By the time he had finished his breakfast, he would be his usual self.

'Wasn't it dark last night, Mum?' He made a statement rather than asked a question.

'Yes, you didn't used to like the dark once. I'm pleased you are more sensible now.' She smiled at him as she remembered the nights when he had tossed and turned and cried out in his sleep, as if trying to escape something only he could see or feel.

Then it was off to school, hurrying along the wet road, with the water and mud splashing up from the tyres of his bike. His coat had been dragged over his school bag to keep it and himself dry in the persistent drizzle. Only a mile. Some of the kids had three of four times as far to go. As he pushed himself along, a vague memory of last night came back, and he said to himself out loud, 'You had a nightmare, you dope.'

The rain had cleared by lunchtime, and the night was cold and clear. The stars were white and friendly in his oblong of light. This night held no terror.

As the years passed, the dark still brought nights of terror. Sometimes he woke, crushed and broken in spirit by the half-remembered torture, with no clear knowledge of what was real and what was conjured up by the blackness of his dreams.

The farm didn't need two men to run it. So, when the owners of the Golden Gleam mine decided to recommence operations, he was given a job there. The mine site was only a few miles into the hills from the farm. It looked for all the world like a rabbit burrow partway up Reef Mountain, with the mullock from the workings spilling down the steep mountainside. Though the work was hard, he was lean and tough, and it gave him no great difficulty.

The six-man team camped at the site for the week and would go their various ways at the weekend, with the exception of Tom. Tom said that the only way he could save his wages was to stay out of town. The rest of the fellows said he'd never spent a penny in his life. It was helpful to have someone to keep an eye on the works, so everyone was happy with the arrangement.

Some of the gang would rib the youngster, because, when it was time to turn in, he would pile an excess of firewood onto the fire at the end of the draughty shed that was their living quarters. He would smile in his quiet, good natured way and make some remark about keeping the home fires burning, or that he liked to be able to keep his eye on certain types that he knew. They didn't object to the extra warmth, and he was comforted by the light from the fire.

One particularly cold, wet night, they had all bedded down earlier than usual, and the fire burned itself out long before morning, leaving him prey to the old terrors of the dark. He lay stiff and motionless in pain and terror that bordered on mind-shattering hysteria. The forgotten nights of the past came crowding into his tortured brain. The realisation that the half-remembered shadows of nightmares were real, brought with it a multiplication of horrors that he had never known, even in the blackest depths of previous despair. He forced himself to remain silent.

When he felt that the agony could be borne no longer, the dark, his enemy, once more engulfed him and his next awareness was the first greyness of morning light. As his numbed brain began to function he dragged on his clothes and began to get the fire going.

'You look like you seen a ghost, mate,' said old Tom as he stuck his head, turtle fashion, from his blankets.

'Just hungry, Tom. I'll be okay when I've had some breakfast.' He gave Tom a half-hearted grin and went out into the cold mountain air, hoping to clear his aching head.

It was different this time. The agony and terror were vividly remembered. His arms ached as if they had been gripped in some gigantic vise. His head throbbed with the pain caused by the nameless something that had tortured him in the quiet blackness.

Working in the Golden Gleam mine may not have had many advantages, but it was warm and dry, something to be appreciated in the winter months. Tom and the youngster were working on the rock face, through which ran the payable, gold-bearing vein. They worked by the light of a couple of globes lit by the battery of the motor-driven winch used to operate the little ore trucks.

The only indication of trouble was when the timbering behind them seemed to explode with a deafening crack. The young man grabbed Tom's arms and spun him around before the veteran had time to move. Tom found himself being literally thrown through the gap between the moving timbers that, with the pressure of the loosening earth, were closing in on them like a trap. He went hurtling along the drive, half rolling, half sliding, to be brought up dazed and bruised against the still undamaged timbers away from the cave-in. As he struggled to his feet, the roof behind him crumbled and collapsed, and in the split second before the lights went out, he saw his young workmate disappear under the avalanche of earth and rock.

Darkness and silence followed the roar of the mine fall. In the choking dust, complete blackness engulfed the young miner. It pressed him down in agony to the floor of the mine, crushing and suffocating him as it swirled and rolled about him in its relentless pressure. There was no terror, and when the physical pain was no longer to be borne, his friend, the dark, enclosed his whole being in its quiet peace.

Tom and the other four workmates took several hours to reach the young man's body. The old man knelt beside it, heedless of the tears coursing through the dust on his cheeks.

'He could have saved himself instead of me, and he wouldn't,' he said over and over. 'He had no fear.'

The Vision Splendid

This story is Dad's tribute to the poem *Clancy of the Overflow* by Banjo Patterson, one of his favourite 'poets of the bush'.

JOE SAT LOOSELY IN the saddle and tried in vain to answer the question he had asked himself a hundred times a day, 'Why did I leave the south-east where the grass is green and the sheep are fat, for this blasted wilderness of dust and skinny cattle, heat and flies, stubborn bosses and greasy camp-cooks, everlasting thirst and empty pockets?'

The sunlit plain extended to the horizon a full three hundred and sixty degrees, and the February sun beat down on his back at least a hundred and thirty degrees. The wind from the north brought the dust, stirred up by the few strays he had herded together, into his sweat-streaked face, and did nothing to improve his thirst, or his temper. A bush rat jumped briskly across in front of his horse, which shook its head sadly, as if to say, 'If I was ten years younger and half as tired I'd shy at that and rid myself of this useless burden on my back.'

It was difficult to say which of the two, horse or rider, looked the more dejected and fed up with the sight and smell of cattle and dust.

As the stock were slowly stringing towards tonight's camp and a drink of bore water, Joe rode behind them whingeing, for a drover's life has frustrations that have to be experienced to be believed.

After years in the saddle, Joe didn't consider himself a tenderfoot, nor did he have a tender heart with regard to cattle, but the saddle was just as hard today as it was yesterday, or last year and would be again tomorrow. No, thought Joe, tenderfoot was not the appropriate term to use for a saddle weary cow nurse. Oh well, the bush had plenty of friends to meet him. Bush, he'd swear there was nothing knee-high to a snake for a hundred miles. You would hardly call the station owner a friend either. Not that Mick Cleary was a bad sort of a bloke. At least he wasn't a King William Street cocky with a manager to run the place. In the first place, he couldn't afford a manager, and even if he could, the land was too miserable to run a manager to a million acres.

Cleary of the Overdraft, they called him, and the only time he ever saw King William Street was when he fronted the manager of the particular bank that held him prisoner on his own land. That was once a year when mounting bills had to be met.

This year, the grazing was so poor that it would take three head of cattle to make a hamburger, and they had to stack themselves up against each other so they wouldn't fall over. They had to gallop from one blade of grass to the next, or it would take them all day to get a mouthful. It was a mere handful of these fine beasts that had taken Joe until mid-afternoon to muster – and fine beasts they certainly were – end on you could hardly see them.

Ho hum, another couple of hours and they could get a drink. As long as the bottom hadn't rusted out of the trough, or the windmill hadn't broken down again – this bore wasn't one of the gushing artesians where the water was pushed to the surface. The clanking, rackety windmill was already in view, floating above the shimmering heat haze that played tricks with the eyes and the imagination. Joe hardly knew whether he was awake or oozing along in a hot, sticky nightmare from which he would soon wake up and find himself under a shady gum tree on the sheep farm where he had grown up, and was stupid enough to leave.

He'd left in in '14 to join the Light Horse, and after four years of heat, cold, dust, mud, horses and hard saddles, the monotony of which was relieved by being either shouted at or shot at, had allowed himself to be talked into taking his present job by his mate, Lofty Johnson.

'Friend of mine called Cleary's got a bonzer spread up north. How about comin' up with me? All ya gotta do is sit on a horse and let it walk around after cows.'

Yeah, he was a mate all right. After three months of mild spring weather, with the temperature hardly ever above a hundred, Lofty had tossed it in and gone back to his daddy's apple orchard in the hills just outside of Adelaide.

Here was Joe after three years of eating bull dust. No wonder you read about the grizzled stockmen, most of them did little else but grizzle, Joe could make a living at it.

The monotony of the seemingly endless plain was changed suddenly by a mighty canyon-like creek-bed, gouged out of the harsh red earth a million years ago, when it had last rained. Maybe it had rained since, Joe wasn't sure.

Where the cattle had to cross was at least two feet deep and four wide. A south-eastern rabbit could have cleared it in its stride. All the cows, with the exception of the last tired Madam Methusalah of a cow, had crossed by the time Joe had dashed up to it at close to walking pace. Well, a slow walk. If old Meth had ever had any spirit, it had completely evaporated in the long walk that hot, tiring day, and now she stood looking sadly into the bottom of the yawning chasm, apparently wishing it were deep enough to swallow her from the sun's pitiless heat.

After careful consideration, she convinced herself that in her condition it was quite impassable, and she stood, swaying slightly, sighing in the anguish of the burden of her years.

Joe uncoiled his stock whip, then reckoned swinging it was too much like hard work, and committed the unforgivable sin of stockmen. He dismounted right alongside his bovine companion.

Now these cattle were half wild and not used to pedestrians. Memories of younger, wilder days stirred in her brain. In her agitation, she flicked one ear but made no other effort to advance or retreat. Joe, in his sweaty, half-awake condition, had not seen the danger signs of possible attack, but approached and gave the old beast a half-hearted slap on the rump with the flat of his hand to urge her over the ditch. The cow moved with such speed that Joe was taken by surprise. Her front hooves shuffled forward a few inches nearer the edge of the ravine, which gave way under her weight. In an instant she was flat on her side, on top of the unhappy cowman.

The sudden movement panicked the riderless horse which, without a backward glance, ambled off in the direction of the windmill, content in its solitude.

Joe reacted, 'Get off me, you blasted overgrown old goat, before I boot your ribs in.' She might have been skinny, but old bones weigh heavy, and she was in no danger of being booted by the angry Joe, because both his legs were firmly trapped under her dusty hide. In falling, they had slid into the creek bed. The old cow's legs were resting on one side and Joe's back against the other. He would have been quite comfortable if he hadn't been nursing a cow on his knees.

She gave a couple of feeble struggles, mooed softly and lay still. Joe gave quite a number of energetic struggles, mooed harshly and unprintably, at great length. Neither the struggling nor the soliloquy had any appreciable effect. His only other alternative was to keep still and shut up. He did. He was not happy. He took careful stock of the situation and saw no humour in it. The cow had Buckley's hope of getting up, and Joe, in his comfortable sitting position, couldn't move in any direction.

True, he could lean forward and bite her on the back, and his hands were free. If any more flies came to the party he would have no fear of sunstroke as they almost blotted out the sun now, and he was still wearing his battered army hat.

To pass a few minutes, he ran through the comprehensive vocabulary of swear words he'd collected during four years of war and three years of cattle. He was multi-lingual. He was stuck. Oh, and he was worried. If his companion in strife was to kick the bucket, as it were, and drift off to her eternal pasture in the sky, Joe's future would not be good.

There were a few hours of hot sunlight left, and no-one was going to be strolling by to give him a hand. Once again, he queried the wisdom of leaving home.

Boy, it was hot. Joe didn't mind a bit of hot weather. In fact, sitting there without the cow, and thirty degrees cooler, would have been quite pleasant. Well, he had been in many awkward situations in his time, and he had a reputation for having plenty of nerve, but right now, if he'd had room to move, he would be shaking in his boots. He tried to work out how long he'd be likely to stay alive. Steak Tartare à la Hoof, and the damned horse had walked off with the water bag.

The heat was making him dizzy, and his legs felt squashed with the weight of the cow, which had given up all hope of ever getting up. She was still alive because Joe could feel her erratic heartbeat against his right knee. Not for much longer – his legs were starting to go numb. His feet hurt and he became a little hysterical at the thought of always having to walk like a ballet dancer, with his feet permanently in line with his legs. How would he look, going into the bar of the Blue Lake pub like a fairy prince – no one would drink with him. Yeah, it'd be real funny, only it wasn't.

'How long have I been here? Maybe two hours, or even longer. The sun's gone down a fair bit.' He folded his arms on the hot, dusty, smelly hide and rested his aching head on them. He was hot, his throat was dry and sore, and he lapsed into a state of semi-consciousness. Even with his eyes closed, he could still see the fiery redness of heat, and waves of delirium engulfed his reeling brain.

'If she dies I'll never get out of it,' and he jerked upright, fully conscious and completely panic-stricken. He beat his fists wildly on the beast's hollow rib cage. The sound echoed inside her like a drum. The futility of his wasted effort came home to him in a wave of despair, and he laid his head once more on his arms. His legs were numb now, and he could no longer feel her heart beating against his knee. 'Then if they are numb, why do they hurt so much, and if they're not numb ...?' The answer to that was stark in its simplicity – she had no heartbeat.

When he lifted his head again, some of the hot fierceness of the day had gone. Turning, he could see the sun resting on the horizon. 'Like a damn great over-ripe tomato on the edge of a dinner plate a hundred miles round – I'm going off my nut.'

There was not a sound, not even a dingo. 'Dingoes,' Joe yelled the word at the top of his voice, but it came out in a hoarse croak, he hadn't thought of them before. 'They don't attack anyone alive, do they?' He twisted his head again just in time to see the last slice of tomato slide off the edge of the plate. There were only him and his steak left.

He opened his mouth and put all his strength into a sound that came out roughly like, 'Help,' and a quiet voice said, 'Yeah, Joe. For you or your pet?'

It was old Jim Clark who had arrived at the bore to find Joe's horse having a quiet drink, and no sign of Joe. 'So, I back-tracked your mob, just to see what you reckoned was more interestin' than my company and a billy of tea. I don't admire your choice,' said Jim. 'If you want to be alone with your friend, I'll be getting back.'

By this time, Jim was off his horse and wetting Joe's throat and burning forehead with the contents of his water bag. The water revived Joe's vocal chords, and he was able to explain to Jim his long, close attachment to his now departed friend. He asked politely if Jim would mind removing the animal from his knees. Jim very much doubted that he was quite up to the task, but he'd certainly try. He soon proved that he was correct in the assessment of his limitations. Joe had not been of any great help in his endeavours, except in an advisory capacity.

'I've got a knife and fork in my roll,' said Jim.

'Bloody comedians like you'd be more use at the Tivoli,' said Joe.

Jim stood back and rubbed his bristly jaw, a grin on his face. 'Well, it's one of Slimey Charlie's butchers knives, and it's sharp. Are you going to carve, or will I?'

The hide was tough and the carcass bony, but Jim reckoned it was one of the best jobs of butcherin' he'd ever done.

The moon was well up by the time Joe was on his feet.

'You've been sittin' round doin' nothin' all afternoon,' said Jim. 'So you won't mind hoofin' it back to the bore while I ride in and get the billy boilin'.'

'I'm never goin' to walk anywhere, anytime, Jim. And that worn out nag of yours won't carry two.'

There wasn't much of the night left by the time the two weary wayfarers hit camp. Tea, stale damper and corned beef never tasted so good. When they were at last on their blankets, who's to blame them if they didn't contemplate the wondrous glory of the everlasting stars? They knew that the cattle wouldn't stray from the bore overnight. They slept.

That night, Joe dreamed of green pastures, deep water and shady trees, and reckoned he'd really had his turn at droving, where the seasons come in hot and go out dusty.

There had been enough dust in his throat to last him a lifetime, and he'd soon see the vision splendid of a foaming glass extended, and at night the wondrous glory of the ever open bars.

North to Paradise

The next two stories, though fictional, draw on Dad's time in Darwin. Dad was posted there for about three years during World War 2, at the time of the bombings. Dad did not like the tropics.

THOSE FIRST FIVE WEEKS in the Territory just about finished me off. Summer in South Australia was pretty warm, I thought, but nothing like the thick, sticky atmosphere of the northern coastal area. It seemed to drag the last ounce of energy out of me, and just to remain more or less upright was effort enough without the added exertion of work. Some people seem to thrive in it, and I suppose anyone can become acclimatized to tropical conditions, eventually. After three wet seasons in the area, I was no more enchanted with the place than when I'd first arrived.

It was late September when I first went north, on a plane trip of unbelievable turbulence. You can fly for hours – now, the same trip takes only a fraction of the time – without seeing any relieving features on the flat eternity of the harsh, sun-baked central plains. You would naturally think that the make-up of the atmosphere would follow the flatness of the country. Oh brother, would you be wrong! Thermals, air pockets, willy-willys of staggering dimensions, stuffed with sand, aided and abetted by the blazing sun, made the trip a nightmare for passengers in the toy planes of the mid-thirties. It was as if we were belting through a carelessly laid out obstacle course.

The morning we took off from the Alice, there was a clear, intensely blue sky, with almost no wind at all. Yet, within a few minutes of leaving the ground we were being battered with such force, you would have been forgiven if you thought that every Kadaitcha man that had ever sung vengeance on his enemies was willing destruction on the aircraft and its occupants. Who is to say they were not?

Johnny Lumm was our pilot on this trip. Lean, wiry and nerveless, his face showed no more strain or stress than if he'd been sitting in his favourite chair at home. He was the only one not adversely affected by the buffeting. Even his co-pilot, mechanic, man-of-all-jobs, Alan Something, looked somewhat dispirited after an hour or two of it. The other three passengers and I were ill.

I'd made a few trips in the southern states before this. My line of business demanded some rapid movement now and then. I considered myself a seasoned air traveller, in the days when there were not many about, but those six hundred (or whatever it is) miles from the Alice to Birdum were worse than any I'd ever put in.

I can't explain why six hundred-odd miles should take nine and a half hours, or how any pilot could keep a little tin-pot plane airborne for so long under those conditions, and at the end of it look as if he'd ridden his bike to the corner shop for the afternoon paper. We only put down once, and if I hadn't been so ill I'd have telegraphed my resignation then and there. Our lunch and refuel stop would have been Tennant Creek, I guess – personally I didn't care where it was, I knew I'd never eat again anyway. I know I was first off and last on again. Even Lummy gave me a sympathetic look as I boarded with great reluctance, clutching the handholds, my briefcase and my stomach all at the same time – you should try it.

Birdum was our night stop, and by the time we got there I knew all about eternity.

I made a wonderfully quick recovery from my air sickness – I suppose sheer funk was the main cause of my illness. I was too young to die. I could have eaten a good breakfast next morning, but lacked the confidence to do so, besides Lummy had said, 'Lunch at the top – be there by twelve, no trouble.'

Strangely enough, take off was the roughest part of the day's trip. I had expected the more broken terrain to create greater thermals, but we were down on the Bay airfield well before noon. From the air, the town on its tree covered peninsular and the white beaches with their sparkling water, were lovely enough to make me realise that this tropical paradise would do me for the next year or two.

Mosquitoes, flies and sand flies can't be easily identified from a couple of thousand feet up – within days I could identify them by their bite.

The 'wet' was still a few weeks away, but even then, the air had the consistency of thick, hot custard, richly impregnated with dust.

Australia's back door – boy what a tradesman's entrance it was then.

Slade himself was there to meet me, but that didn't make me think I was super important. I knew he'd be there to make sure I didn't do anything too damn stupid.

I'd forgotten how much I disliked him until I saw him standing comfortably at ease, just out of the meagre shade of the straggly, colourless trees beside the airstrip. Slade wouldn't have lowered his dignity so much as to seek shade. He'd be no more likely to sweat in the tropics than he would be to shiver in the Antarctic.

Too long in the Navy, that was Slade's trouble. Trouble to other ranks, not to himself.

Two years ago, I'd seen him standing like that on Station Pier. Tall, straight, broad, expressionless – just about as friendly and outgoing as the Sphinx. Then, he'd worn navy blues, now he was in white – spotless of course.

'Nugent,' he growled, with such a show of cordiality that I was afraid he'd kiss me. 'Let's go,' he said as he opened the car door and got in, leaving me to take whatever choice of seats I wanted, as long as it wasn't beside him. I got in beside the driver because Slade had already, quite deliberately, closed the rear door anyway.

There was plenty of room for my bag and my feet in the front – if I wore size ones instead of size nines. For one reckless moment I considered tossing my luggage onto the back seat beside Slade. He probably wouldn't have said anything, and I doubt whether he was armed. It wasn't that he disliked me, in all fairness he treated everyone alike – as though they didn't exist.

The dusty drive from the airfield to H.Q. didn't take long. I felt thirsty as we passed the rain- and sun-weathered pub near the narrows. Anyone except Slade would have settled some of the dust there. The driver and I were mentally in communication with each other, but remained silent and dry. There was a 'Puffing Billy' style steam train panting in a state of near exhaustion in the railway yards, and it was getting a drink.

Then we were through the town and turning into Slade's kingdom.

Slade said, 'Shower, lunch, and in my office at 1.30.' I was about to suggest synchronising watches, but he went on to the driver. 'Take Nugent to B-section, Petty Officer Clarke knows where he's to go,' and he left.

The driver relaxed all over, grinned at me and said, 'Jackson's my name, sir. If there's anything I can do, just say. You must have known the boss a while to get so matey with him.' Jackson was a solid little chap, red-headed and shouldn't have been exposed to the tropical sun, or been away from his mother, judging by his boyish face. However, he had a look of cheerful confidence about him. The navy would make a good reliable shipmate out of him, but never a Slade.

I stuck out my hand and said, 'Glad to know you, sailor. I don't rate a 'sir' though. I'm *ex*-navy. Slade calls me Nugent, strangers call me Mister Nugent, other ranks usually call me Nugget.'

'Welcome aboard, Mister Nugent,' he said politely. Then the friendly grin took over again, 'Well, we haven't known each other for that long.'

He drove between the louvred fibro-cement buildings of Slade's kingdom and stopped in front of one. I had the car door already open so he wouldn't jump out and play the boss's driver for me.

'You'll find Petty Officer Clarke in there. Like the boss said, he'll tell you where to go.' I'd been a P.O. for many years, and guessed Jackson meant what he said.

I opened the office door quietly. My wonderful powers of deduction told me that P.O. Clarke wasn't expecting Slade and me back yet. His feet were resting comfortably on the desk, the chair tilted back on two legs, and no doubt he was dreaming of pleasant places far away. I stood in front of him for a few seconds wondering what was going on in the Navy since I'd left and then bellowed at the top of my voice in traditional P.O. manner, 'CLARKE!'

As he picked himself up, still recovering from the fright, he took a long, unbelieving look at me. The stupid look slowly changed to a broad grin – everything about his battered face was broad – and he stooped to me in the eye – I'm only about six feet tall. 'Nugget, you old pirate. This miserable, flea-bitten, over-heated backwash of a town will never be the same after we've finished with it.'

He stepped from behind the desk, grabbed me by the arms, hoisted me clear of the floor and sat me down too solidly on the desk, scattering papers pens and pencils onto the floor. 'You were always a puny kid. I could still take you with one hand.'

'The only reason you're still in the Navy and I'm out of it is because you have to have someone to look after you,' I told him.

His grinning face was beautiful only in its friendliness. Defence must have been his big weakness in his boxing days. If that was a nose, I didn't want one, and cauliflowers the size of his ears would have brought top price at the Vic Market. I still shudder when I remember playing full-forward against him when his ship and mine were in together, five or six years back. At least I was faster than he was. I had to be.

'Look, give me a hand to tidy up this mess. I'm expecting some stiff shirt from Intelligence any minute, and I need to make a good impression or His Majesty will throw me to the sharks. I'll get rid of the drongo as soon as I can, and you can tell me what winds of utter disaster blew you into this hole.'

We picked up the scattered contents of the desk, and he went on. 'Naval Intelligence, hah! you can imagine how intelligent he'll have to be, to be exiled to this paradise – he's probably scuttled a battleship and this posting is his reward.'

The office was ship-shape once more, so I said, 'Slade said you'd show me to my quarters.'

'Sure, Nugget, straight through the front gate, second street right and the little Chinese cafe a couple of doors from the Joss house. You'll find the cutest little waitress you ever laid eyes ... Slade what? You're kidding. You're Naval Intelligence? You're not even intelligent. The navy is in worse shape than I thought. Naval Intelligence, wow!'

'You're right there, Buster. I arrive secretly in civvies, intending to move into a pub under-cover, and your brilliant leader meets me as though I'm the governor-general. The Navy has an epidemic of intelligence on its hands. You're lucky you've built up an immunity.'

Then I remembered, 'shower, lunch, 1:30'. 'I've got to see our little playmate at half-past-one, so find me a room with a view and a bite to eat, an anti-Slade injection, or a rabies shot, so I can face the hound in his own little kennel. You'll keep for later on.'

Slade had company at 1:30. 'Colonel Davidson, Squadron Leader Gregory,' said Slade by way of greeting, indicating each in turn with a nod. Then a nod in my direction, '... Nugent. We know why you're here, Nugent, and we will co-operate. Technically you are Naval personnel and under my command.'

I'm a mild type and said, 'Yessir,' which, roughly translated meant, 'That's what you think.'

Davidson was close to retiring age, overweight, florid, 'Any assistance we can, Nugent.' Whisky and cigars hadn't helped his diction.

Gregory looked like a university professor. The direct, blue-eyed look he gave me was searching but friendly, and said exactly the same as Davidson, but without speaking. 'I'd have thought you'd have come in unannounced, Mr Nugent, and stayed undercover as long as you could.'

He was even more mild and gentle than I.

'It's not always possible, sir.' I must get out of the habit of calling officers, 'sir', but after twelve years of rapid promotion to P.O. it wasn't easy. 'Whatever course of action you gentlemen suggest will be quite satisfactory, I'm sure.'

The blue eyes under the thinning, blonde hair had a distinct twinkle in them, and I knew I could count on full air support. Army and Navy had formed an alliance, but Intelligence was against them.

'No Navy personnel were involved.' A flat statement, and no room for doubt or argument, and for some reason the contrasting countenances of Clarke and Jackson came into my mind. Those two wouldn't do such a thing, not without Intelligence – sorry, small 'i' – to guide them. I wonder why he mentioned the Chinese café – oh yes, the waitress.

I was aware of Davidson's assurance that his men were absolutely sound, morale high, discipline rigid – I knew he was longing for a scotch, but the only cool thing in the office was Slade's attitude – a beer would go extremely well – besides I wanted to think things out, and I said, 'With the serious branches of the fighting forces exonerated, what are we left with?'

'Mr Nugent?' Gregory's mouth, as well as the eyes, smiled. 'Oh, I'm sure the Air Force is above suspicion, sir.' Somehow, Gregory didn't seem to be taking the matter quite as seriously as Davidson and Slade.

Why did I keep on seeing Clarke? 'He'll tell you where to go.' That was it, he knew damn well why I was there. Possibly indirectly, Slade had told him. So much for secrecy.

I knew Buster had laid his Petty Officership on the line more than once, even in my company – I was easily led – but I was sure he was no traitor, and Jackson, so open and candid. Yet, they knew something about it.

I pulled myself together and realised the others were talking. Davidson was going on about the possibility of the hospital staff not being all it could be, and I knew Gregory wanted to laugh outright as he made the observation that he considered the hospital staff everything it could be. Later, when I met Nurse Hanson, I knew what he meant – she sure was everything she could be.

The Army and the Navy were less expressive in countenance than ever, and Slade closed the meeting with 'It's your job, Nugent. Work it out.'

Davidson said he was late for an appointment, and I guessed it was with J. Walker, late of the Highland Regiment. Gregory said there were a couple of things he might be able to help me with, so we left the allies to their jokes and high spirits and went out. Once outside, Gregory gave a hearty chuckle and said, 'You're not Nugget Nugent by any chance, are you?'

'My fame goes before me. How did you know?' I forgot to say 'sir'.

'Oh, I know Buster, and when I heard those nice little "yessirs" and "I agree, sir", I knew who you were. Buster reckons you're the only man who ever put him on his back.'

'He tripped over me,' I said.

'Do you have to get on with the job straight away, or would you like to start investigations at the Raff? It's not so dusty there.'

He read my throat like a book, and I accepted his invitation. He had a most unregimental vehicle that had been, and still slightly resembled, a Model A roadster in which we bounced out to the Air Force base, just out of town. Soon, I was feeling much better than I'd felt since leaving the Alice, and the throat infection was completely gone.

But, there was work to do, a job to be done, and I was the unsentimental, tough agent to make wrong right and bring just deserts to lawbreakers. I'd been told by Admiral Harvey in Melbourne not to involve the civil authorities. 'They're cops, you know.' So I said to Gregory, forgetting the 'sir' again, 'What do you know about it, Johnny?'

'Nothing really, except that it happened. Valuable Defence Department property, just gone. You've got to be careful where you start fooling around and if word gets around ...'

I knew what he meant. I wasn't dealing with the Girl Guides. 'Buster knows more people in town than anyone. I know he'll help you. At least you can trust him.'

'I might need transport. Do you know where I can get a car?'

He jerked his thumb in the direction of the window and his jalopy and said, 'Pull to start, push to stop. Watch it though if you have to use the starting handle.'

He wouldn't listen to my refusal. 'Perfect cover, Nugget. No one intelligent would drive it,' and with mock dignity, 'Besides, I have a staff car.'

I knew what he meant the first time I got caught in the rain in it.

The afternoon was disappearing. With my throat trouble cured had come the desire to beat some information out of Buster. So, thanking Gregory for the beer and the car, in order of importance, I chugged back to my billet.

Movement gave some relief from the sticky heat. I noticed a long low bank of cloud out over the sea, with lightning flickering almost continually. I wasn't challenged at the pearly gate of Slade's kingdom, unless you called a friendly lift of the hand from the rating on sentry-go a challenge.

I pulled up a few yards past Buster's office. I'd meant to stop at the door but hadn't had reason to use the brakes before. One of the first things you should do when you borrow a car is test the brakes.

Buster was awake, as it was knock-off time. Half a million square miles of territory was within bounds until midnight, and my host suggested a Chinese café.

The waitress was more than cute. Alongside Buster she looked tiny, but she was above average height, small boned and as graceful in her movements as a ballerina.

A gazelle and a water buffalo would have been a better pair, but it was obvious that they didn't think so. Even her soft, gentle voice was in complete contrast to his. He could out-bellow the roughest gale. Her slight accent added to the attraction of her near perfect

English. Her first name was translated as Melody. It suited her.

Buster introduced me as a friend from down south who'd had to get out of the Navy. She giggled and said what a terrible man I must be, as Buster was still in it. Buster threatened her with dire punishment, but the enormous paw he put on her arm was gentle.

My wild friend was tamed for sure. As we left the café, he said, 'What do you think of her?'

'I know why you've gone soft in the head, and you know why I'm here. You didn't want to believe I'd been sent up to investigate. We've been friends for a long time, Buster, but if you're in on this deal, you'll get the same treatment from me as if you were Slade gone bad.'

The kitten caressing paw with which he'd held Melody's arm came down on my shoulder but no longer gentle. I thought the bones would break. If he'd increased the pressure I was going to remind him that I was the only man who could put him on his back. Maybe he didn't need reminding, and said as softly as ten tons of gravel sliding off a truck, 'The little kid's mixing it with the big league, put your hand up if you get in deep water. Uncle Buster will wade in and drag you out.'

The squeeze of the big hand was gentle and friendly, and I hated the job I had to get on with. He had changed though.

Previously, whenever we met after being parted for a spell, we'd celebrate, and with Buster celebrating, anything could happen. Like the night he locked two policemen in their wagon in Carlton, drove them out to Mordialloc and returned to the city by taxi with the distributor cap of the police car. He kindly called into Russell Street, Police Headquarters, and left it there for them.

Admittedly, I'd been with him but had nothing to do with it. Mostly, he liked cops but I don't think he liked the idea of me being one – well sort of one. After a beer or two, or maybe three, he said I must be tired and we were going to a dance at the Raff tomorrow night and Gregory would have some hospital staff for me to question. 'Go to bed, sonny,' he said.

I showered and crawled under my mosquito net and was asleep immediately.

It was two or three in the morning when I woke, hot and clammy and stifled. Then the impact of Buster's last remark hit me. I should have counted the beers. Johnny Gregory had been in touch with Buster between the time I left Raff and my arrival at Naval H.Q, a matter of a few minutes. I didn't want to believe they were both in on it. I liked them both too much, and I wondered if I could hand in my resignation to Slade – technically my commanding officer – or should I telegraph south? Then they'd send a Slade type who would say 'yessir' and methodically tear my oldest, and newest, friends to pieces. 'It would look very bad if no disciplinary action was taken. After all, morale in a key defence position such as this ...' – 'Yessir, I agree sir'.

Buster loved the Navy, and Melody. Melody, what did she know? The Asian influence up here was pretty strong. Buster was wild and tough, Gregory intelligent and shrewd, but Melody soft, gentle, graceful. Yes, she was a really nice girl, and I knew she had nothing to do with it.

I lay awake in a sweat until dawn; there hadn't been much change in temperature all night. I got up, showered and then had breakfast in the mess with Buster.

Whatever he had on his mind didn't affect his appetite. I was hungry too.

I restricted my movement to taking showers and dodging Slade all morning. After lunch, I disguised myself as a Navy Intelligence Investigative Officer and took a tour around the wharf area, railway yards, even the rusting meat works, and anywhere else I reckoned Slade wouldn't be. I was expecting him to summon me to his lair, but heard nothing from him.

Buster and I ate at the cafe again, and as we were leaving he said to Melody, 'I'll pick you up at eight.'

That night, we somehow squeezed into Gregory's car and rattled out to the Raff, where the mess hall had been cleared for a dance.

Johnny came over to me as soon as we walked inside. His 'Hello, Mel,' made me realise they were old friends. To Buster he said, 'I'll fight you for her any time – choose your weapons.' Buster grinned and waved a fist the size of a Christmas pudding under his nose and said, 'Bring on your machine guns, Johnny boy.'

I don't know what had happened to protocol – a P.O. on such familiar terms with the Squadron Leader. Then I wished I hadn't thought that – just how familiar were they?

I didn't stand there wool gathering for long because a carload of hospital staff arrived right then, and Gregory was saying, 'Nugget, this is Janet Hanson.' Nurse Janet Hanson, like Johnny had said, was everything she could be. I rocked back a little on my heels when she said 'Hello Nugget. I've been looking forward to meeting you. How are the investigations coming along?' Her big grey eyes were mocking and there was a teasing tone in her voice.

'Some secret agent,' I thought. 'All the nicest people in the place are in on this thing.' I had my resignation word perfect.

But there were more important things to consider, like the little sprinkling of freckles on Nurse Janet Hanson's nose, and the softness of her hair that reached my chin when we danced, and that trick of looking up through long eyelashes when she laughed, and the honest level gaze of her big, grey eyes.

Later in the evening, I said to Buster, 'Look, little man, I don't care how you and Melody get back to town. I've got a job to do. You know what it is and you know I'll follow it through to whatever end it leads – anyone in the road will have to stop me or get walked on. Someone is out to wreck morale, and the careers of all the officers in the area, and defence can't afford that to happen. I think you know who is to blame, and I think you and your friends could fix the wrong that's been done.'

Johnny drove Buster and Melody back to town after the dance. I had some questions to put to Nurse Janet Hanson that had nothing to do with Navy, Army or Air Force.

Slade called me into his office next morning, immediately after breakfast.

'Everything has been returned – absolutely nothing is missing.' Then emotion got the better of him at last, and with almost a movement of his firm mouth, 'Thanks, Nugent.'

I was still puzzled, and as I handed my resignation to him I was trying to figure out how they ever got a truck load of assorted spirits back to each of three Officers Messes without being seen.

So how did I end up spending three wet seasons there? Well, my investigations along the waterfront had turned up an advertisement for a shipping clerk, single, accommodation provided. So, I applied for the job and got it.

It was only coincidence that Nurse Janet Hanson had signed on at the hospital for three years. She said she wouldn't marry me until we went south when the three years were up.

Return to the North

H**AVING CLEARED UP THE** matter of the missing booze, I resigned from the Department of the Navy and settled down to the mundane existence of noting what came and went on ships. Take notice that I said what, not who. Maybe the life of a shipping clerk in a northern tropic clime is less exciting than that of an undercover investigator of things that go wump in the Navy, but at that time, it was just what I needed to calm my frayed nerves and allow my trauma-infested gray cells to settle down to some degree of normality. Normal for me, I mean, not for the average, well-adjusted, efficient shipping clerk.

Let it be understood that I never, at any time, approved of civilised persons living within a thousand miles of what might be termed the back door of Australia. If I am ever called upon to serve a term in purgatory, please let it not be along Australia's northern shoreline.

During my long, irksome career in the Silent Service, I had the pleasure of crossing both the Arctic and Antarctic Circles, and though some of the night watches were far from comfortable, I found them more bearable than the mosquito-laden humidity of Tropical land bases.

Well then, you may ask, why would I take on a lowly clerking job under the thunderheads of Tropicana, when I could have done the same job, and collected the same pay, in that wonderful, beautiful City of Churches, with its friendly people and mild climate. You may have diplomatically skipped any mention of white frost and days of one-hundred-degree heat, but the answer I'd give to your question would be, 'a pair of sparkling eyes'.

Grey, level, honest, searching eyes in a sun-tanned face, under a sleek, pale corn sheaf of smooth, shining hair, and a nose with no more, and no less, than its fair share of freckles. All this and much more belonged to Nurse Janet Hanson.

I, the impervious, the indestructible, the lone wolf, the confirmed bachelor, had crumbled, melted – damn the weather, that's the wrong word. But I had refused to run, and it had taken just one glance from those grey eyes to make me realise that life as I had known it had ceased to exist, and life had begun. For me to accept, in fact happily embrace, life in the steamy north, rather than be separated from she who had become my life, was indeed proof of my complete capitulation. She had recently signed away three years of her young life to become a ministering angel of mercy in this sun-girt town. May I also add rain-girt, wind-girt, fly-girt and heat-girt. This I accepted for the love of a lady.

I said to her one day, 'But they'd let you go if we got married,' and to myself added, 'and you can bite off your tongue, Nugget Nugent.'

She said to me, 'You wouldn't want me not to keep my agreement.' It wasn't even a question, so I didn't have to answer.

She quickly let me know that there would be no wedding bells ringing in my ears for the best part of three years yet, if I wanted her to be Mrs Nugent. That's what I wanted. 'But, dear, I am nearly as old as the twentieth century.'

'Then another two and a bit years longer won't make that much difference.' The freckles crinkled and the eyes laughed at me, and I laughed with the sheer joy of loving. There wasn't much I could say.

I had arrived in the humidity of the approaching wet season, and then Christmas had thundered in, booming and flashing across the harbour, echoing back from the low-lying hinterland. Creeks became muddy torrents, plains became lakes, and the town became an island, approachable only by sea. The track – 'road' would have been an exaggeration – had mired into a sea of quag and the railway line was so deep in water that the fireman on the locomotive had to wear diving gear. Necessity could have invented the steam submarine.

I had become the proud owner of a long-handled shovel and an Model A roadster, formerly the possessions of Johnny Gregory, R.A.A.F. No one went anywhere by car in those days without a shovel, either to dig yourself out, or to bury the damned thing. Touring conditions were not ideal there in the late thirties. Johnny had said, 'Well, you use the blasted thing more than I do, and I do have a staff car at my disposal.' The lordly look he tried to adopt didn't fit the devil-may-care gleam in his eyes. 'Give me your next couple of pay cheques and she's yours, even the bottle of Johnny Walker under the front seat – didn't know that was there, did you?' he added with a grin.

'You didn't know it's now only half a bottle, but thanks anyway.'

I'd have perished there without the car. The fact is that I very nearly perished because of it more than once, but it was high and sturdy, and it was possible to travel the streets of the town in it, even in the wet.

The best restaurant in town, you could almost count them on your thumbs, was run by one of the most lovable rogues I've ever known, and I was fortunate in having a room behind it – well, sort of a room, but let's face it, in the wet, nothing keeps the weather out, and in the dry, nobody cares. So, I was as comfortable as the circumstances would permit. The restaurateur's daughter had, as Sister Hanson had done to me, tamed the wildest beast in the R.A.N. namely, the much battered, Buster Clarke. He had blacked my eye and I had bloodied his nose the first day we met at school. Ever since, we had been inseparable friends, to the embarrassment of our parents, and the detriment of the nation. He was huge and ugly, and I loved him like a brother.

When in the company of his beloved Melody he was a veritable Little Lord Whats-it. Melody and Janet realised their foolishness in allowing the terrible twins to continue to associate, but even the good influence that they undoubtedly had on our lives couldn't quite quell our adventurous spirits, and there was no one around to tame the cherubic A. B. Jackson, that bland infant who held the exalted position of driver to Slade, R.A.N. Sorry, sir, Captain Slade.

On duty, Jacko was the perfect example of navy personnel, smooth, clean and shiny, and one was inclined to despair that he had been torn away from the loving care of his mother at such an early age. Red curls, blue eyes and fair complexion not yet ruined by the ravages of the great north. Off duty, he was a pirate, buckling with the swashest, with the gleam of battle blazing in the wide, wild blur of his eyes. On his sweet countenance for the world to read in fear and trembling, his motto, 'I will not obey.' This indeed was a wild colonial boy.

Secrets are hard to keep in the navy, even by the high and mighty, and despite the many questions and suggestions as to the origin of

Slade, Jacko somehow discovered that the great man was about to celebrate his fiftieth birthday.

We four, Buster, Jacko, Johnny Gregory and I, were eating at the restaurant.

'Hey, can't we give Slade a party?' says Jacko. 'Just a little something to remember us by.'

Buster had his own ideas as to what the celebration should involve, but moral, civil, and Naval laws prevented the execution of them. Johnny couldn't imagine the great man at a party. 'Slade, Bligh and Buster Keaton could all sit around all night drinking champagne and giggling.' I saw the gleam in Jacko's eye and paled visibly. I was in bad company, in fact the very best of bad company.

Jacko turned to me and I gave an audible sigh of relief as he changed the subject. 'How's the car going, Nugget?'

'Great, the plugs out of Slade's car made mine a new one. I hope you remembered to thank him for them.'

'He's got plenty. I found some nearly new ones in the garage to replace them. Have you had the hood fixed?'

I told him that canvas wasn't as easy to come by as when Slade joined the navy.

'B-Bligh studied under the ...' he hesitated as Melody approached with our food. When she had gone he said, 'It must be crook driving around without a hood.' I said I liked fresh air.

'And water,' said Johnny.

'Ever given Slade a ride in it?' asked Jacko.

Buster threw back his head and roared at the vision of the immaculate Slade bouncing along in the jalopy. It was a joke.

'Ride, walk or die Slade would choose ride last – especially with me in my car.'

'But wouldn't you like to drive him around town for his birthday?'

The sweet, gentle boy loved his old skipper.

'Yes, I'd love to, but unfortunately his birthday is Friday and the company considers me indispensable,' I told him.

'Will you lend Buster your car? He works the payroll on Thursday night and has Friday afternoon off,' said Jacko.

'You don't have to tell me that,' I said. 'Thanks to his Friday jaunts, the springs are so far down on the driver's side now, I have to tie myself in.'

'That's settled then, Buster can drive him,' said Jackson.

'You've been out in the sun too much, sonny,' rumbled Buster. 'Can't you just imagine me going into the inner sanctum, "Happy birthday dear Slady. Uncle Buster is going to take you for a nice ride around town to cheer up the peasants".'

'I bet you a quid I can get him in the car with you,' said Jacko, the big-time gambler.

'Just tell me how, and I'll feed you here for a week,' offered the big-hearted Buster.

'Fridays, at one-thirty, my beloved master goes out to the station at the Cliffs and no wild tempest will prevent him.' Jacko informed us. 'All you have to do is jog along in your little blue roadster at two o'clock and offer him a lift. He'll be at the narrows expecting you.'

'You're mad,' said Buster.

'Will you do it?' asked the intrepid driver.

'You know what's been happening at two o'clock this week, last week and into the foreseeable future? Hasn't it been wet, Mr Clarke?' asked Jacko in the mildest of tones.

The rain started about one o'clock on Friday afternoon. It thundered down on the roof of my office in a deafening cascade, a solid wall that leaned this way and that with the flurries of a minor gale.

At two, there was a brief respite when the deluge slackened off to a mere, damned heavy downpour.

A familiar chugging, clattering racket made me go to the streaming window, and there, passing by in all his glory, was a grinning, but very wet Chief Petty Officer Milton Clarke at the wheel of my car, and beside him, like a sodden, bedraggled sphinx, erect and looking neither right nor left, was the Birthday Boy. Not by the batting of an eye would he show any sign of discomfort or embarrassment. In spite of myself I had to admire the gallant captain.

Evening brought the end of a week's work and the emptying of the sky of its excess water. We four gathered again at the restaurant. The other three were seated when I arrived and were all wiping tears of laughter from their eyes.

'Able Seaman Jackson, will you please explain …' I got no further as I joined their idiotic laughter. The following is roughly what had taken place.

Slade made his customary inspection of the Cliffs station. Inspection took eleven minutes and at the conclusion of the twelfth minute, Driver Jackson was standing with one hand holding a large umbrella and the other holding the car door, to give the captain access to the back seat. At one thirty, just as they were passing the narrows they came up behind a truck slowly heading for town. By this time the deluge was at its peak.

As if he had read the script, Slade said, 'Overtake him – get me to the wharf by two-thirty.' Just as his driver drew level with the slow-going truck, it slewed across the muddy road. Jackson did his very best to avoid contact with the truck, but the car skidded out of control into the roadside ditch with the front wheels in the ooze, and the chassis firmly grounded amidships. The truck driver, obviously unaware of the mishap, chugged slowly off into the enveloping rain.

'Terribly sorry, sir,' said the contrite driver. 'The other fellow's to blame.'

'Did you get his number?' from Slade.

'I'm afraid it was covered in mud, if it had a number at all, sir,' said Jackson.

They sat without speaking for a few moments, then Jackson said, 'I think I can hear another car coming sir.'

Slade glanced at his watch, 'Two o'clock. Hail him.'

An order is an order, and the driver opened the door with some difficulty and scrambled out into almost knee-deep slush and water as C.P.O. Clarke slithered to a stop some distance from the stranded car. Those brakes still need attention.

'Captain Slade, sir, are you all right?' roared the enormous chief. 'Can I offer you a ride, sir?'

'Get me to the wharf, Clarke,' snapped the captain, and not waiting for his ever-courteous driver to open doors for him, he quickly transferred himself from the comfortable sedan to the wet, uncomfortable roadster. 'Stay with the car, Jackson. I'll send a truck back.'

'Yes, Sir,' said Jackson.

Captain and Petty Officer steered a wet course into town as rapidly as the worsening conditions would permit. There was a noticeable lack of conversation, but the driving rain caused the driver of the vehicle to choke quite badly a couple of times. The motor spluttered several times, and the worried looking Clarke said, 'Nugent's car, sir. He said it was a bit low on petrol and I'm afraid I forgot to put any in.'

That necessitated a drive along the main street, and when he passed one garage, and then another, Slade could no longer remain silent. 'Petrol, Clarke.'

'Yes, Sir, I don't have any money with me, so I'll have to call in to the base and get some from my room,' explained the soaking giant. That meant a short tour of Slade's kingdom that couldn't be helped. Having purchased petrol, after another turn through the town, they headed for the wharf, passing my office on the way. Much to Slade's disgust they reached their destination ten minutes late for his appointment.

By the time the story had been told, Jacko and Buster were helpless. 'He – he never even said thank you,' gasped Buster.

Johnny said, 'You forgot to say happy birthday.'

As we were leaving the restaurant, still laughing like schoolboys a battered old truck pulled up and a tall young fellow got out. 'Hey, Mel,' called out Jacko, 'Jimmy's going to eat here for a week at Buster's expense.'

The rain had started again.

That's the Spirit

OF COURSE THERE ARE ghosts, at least the ones I've spoken to have assured me that there are. It's just that they are not all that easy to get to know.

One of the reasons that people don't believe in them is that they are, in spite of what they might say, afraid of them. So they look the other way when they see one coming and say, 'Oh, there's no such thing,' and having dismissed the idea of their existence, the poor ghost has no other course but to disappear.

The ghosts even believe in ghosts of ghosts. I heard one say one day, 'I saw the ghost of Bogong Harry's ghost the other day, just as sure as you're not standing there, and I know he retired from ghosting over a hundred years ago. Yet there he wasn't, as vaguely as you're not. He's taken up smoking, too. If ever there was a cool ghost in his time it was him – it was he? Even after he disappeared I knew he was for unreal.'

It was during a scramble in the Bogong mountains that I first met a ghost. We'd been camping out a couple of nights and were quite pleased to come across the opening to a cave a couple of hundred feet below the summit of a bushy, rock-strewn mountain top. It had just started to rain and looked like it might get heavy, and sleeping out was not going to be pleasant. Len Warner and Oxy Hammond were with me on this trip, and as it was near sunset, Oxy lit a fire just inside the cave entrance, and Len started preparing a damper. It was my night off, so I poked around in the cave with my flashlight, just to see what I could find. Apart from a few moths on the roof – or ceiling – and a plentiful scattering of bones on the floor – nothing.

The floor was reasonably level, except where it ran up steeply at the back, some hundred feet from the entrance. It might have been forty-odd feet at the widest part and the maximum height, twenty-five. Nearly all the area was high enough to stand upright and half way along on the right as we entered, there was a jumble of rocks which would still be there after tea, so I decided to leave them until then.

After tea, I said, 'I'll be having a look in that pile of rocks.' We had already discussed the old dusty bone deposits and had assumed it had been a popular picnic spot for Aborigines. Anyway, I picked up my flashlight and made my way to the rock pile and thought Len had come with me, because I could hear his footsteps right behind me. He moaned softly, which wasn't unusual. 'There's a packet of *Quickuns* in my pack. I always have a couple after your damper – you know what they say – 'Damper time is time for *Quickuns*'."

He wasn't amused at my ready wit and said nothing, but reached forward over my shoulder and gave me a playful – I hope – slap on the cheek.

'Your hand's as cold as ice, don't tell me you washed up in that cold spring water. You'd need boiling water to get the damper off the plates.'

Once again, my repartee was beneath his utterance. By this time, I'd scrambled around behind the rocks and found a small extension of the cave running in about ten feet and about five feet wide and high. Right at the back were the remains of someone who had eaten too much of Len's damper sometime early this century or last. 'It' was lying on its back, hands caressing the departed damper, and by the expression on the skull, or whatever you call the part that has an expression, it must have been a daddy of a damper pain that took him when he went.

I wasn't used to meeting people in that condition and just stood looking at him for a few moments until good sense told me I was too late for him to do me any harm. My back was aching from the crouched position and my head hurt because I'd tried to stand upright when I first met him.

I respectfully went on to my knees because I couldn't reach him any other way and reached out with my left hand and touched the white bowling ball looking thing which disintegrated at my touch.

Len's voice said at my shoulder, 'Hey, that's mine.'

And I answered without even turning, 'Why the hell aren't you wearing it then?'

His voice sounded hollow and echoey, but caves play audio tricks. 'Anyway,' I said, 'I saw it first, so it's mine.'

The voice said, 'You can't see your own until after, stupid.' I turned to agree that he had a good point there and saw nobody, because I'd forgotten to turn the flashlight as well as my head. So I turned it and was somewhat jolted when I still saw no one.

A very strange, shaky voice said, 'L-Len.' At first, I didn't recognise the shaky voice as mine. No-one answered, and I said in a slightly louder voice, an octave higher than normal, and with a volume equal to a couple of steam train whistles, '*Le-en*!'

From the vicinity of the camp fire Len's voice said, 'Shut up and let me go to sleep.'

'How did you get back there so quick?' I yelled.

'Easy mate, I never left. Now shut up and stop your fooling.'

I wasn't feeling very well and didn't improve any when a voice beside me said, 'You'd scare the dead yelling like that. I only stayed here because it was so peaceful – and look what you've done to my skull. Lucky it only had sentimental value.'

I hadn't started to recover as I flashed the torch all around, up and down, and not seeing anything but rocks and bones, repeated the performance. 'Where are you, what are you, who are you?' I sort of stammered out.

Logic made it clear to me that there was a simple explanation like Oxy playing tricks on me, only I could hear his unmistakable snores from the fireside – no cricket on the hearth, our Oxy. Or I'd flipped – yes that was it.

'How about trying one question at a time and switching that damned thing off, it's a bit sudden, after all the darkness.' I don't know why, but I switched off the torch. 'That's better. I'm my ghost, actually. You'd be able to see me if you only believed in ghosts, but I can see you don't.'

'Oh, come off it, who are you and what's going on?' Anger overcame my fear – a bit.

'Well, my name is – or should I say 'was', no, I guess once a name always a name – is, Jack Peters. I was prospecting up here in '65 – eighteen-sixty-five, that is. Unfortunately, I chose to sleep in this cave without getting permission from the rightful owners. My campfire was right up where yours is – it's quite a good spot. Some trick of the air currents takes the smoke out instead of in. Anyway, I woke up quite suddenly to find the landlords standing over me, and I was wearing a couple of stone spearheads in my bread basket and felt most uncomfortable.

'Well, all I could think of doing on the spur of the moment was to let out a yell, something like you did a while back, and the two nightwatchmen shot through.

'I managed to drag myself into the back of the cave, but didn't last long. The spearheads are probably still under my hands – they were pretty painful, if I remember rightly. I've never liked to look for them, but I'm sure you'd find them there if you cared to try. They don't hurt anymore.

'The Aborigines came back a few times, but after I said 'boo' in their ears just as they were dropping off to sleep, they'd leave, and after a while, stopped calling altogether. They could see me, of course, because they have been well instructed. It was quite amusing once or twice when I let them catch me in broad daylight. I had a bit of trouble at first because I'd try to pick something up and I still had the habit of ducking my head so as not to run into the roof of the cave. My real head has always been where you found it but I kept well away from it for quite a while. It all took some getting used to.'

I still wasn't feeling too good and wondered if he'd mind if I went back to camp. I said I'd like a shot of spirits before I turned in. 'So you do believe,' he said. I told him I meant scotch and he told me he'd been a Pom. He was getting as muddled as I was. I switched on my torch again and still found nothing, so I started back to the camp fire, feeling relieved to be walking away from him and his bones.

I was just about back to the camp when, ahead of me, somewhere in the locality of Len's left ear, I heard a loud 'boo', and the sleeper shot up to a sitting position and tried to keep on coming up. His sleeping bag made that difficult, and he fell quite heavily where he should have stayed sitting.

'You dopey clot, what's got into you tonight?' He was quite angry and his temper didn't improve when I tried to tell him it wasn't me. 'Well?' a voice whispered in my ear. I turned and looked him up and down. He was tall, hefty and bearded and looked much better with everything on. His blue eyes twinkled with the joy of – whatever it is – and he was visibly – good word that – amused at my embarrassment. Len was lying on his side, tenderly rubbing an invisible bruise and muttering about stupid idiots going around acting the fool, like school kids, and that he had indigestion. He usually didn't mention it after he'd done the cooking.

I said, 'Okay, Peters. But you can't blame me, can you? Anyway, it's good to see you.'

I held out my hand to him and felt stupid. He grinned and said, 'I'll make myself scarce and you can get some sleep. You look as though you need it – you look as though you've seen a ghost.' Then he was gone. I don't mean he went away, he was just gone.

I had a stiff scotch, wishing I wouldn't think about stiff Scots, and crawled into my sleeping bag. Len said, 'If you've stopped talking to yourself, I'll try to get some sleep – wouldn't mind a quick one though.' I rolled over and tossed him the packet. 'Scotch, blast you.' So I carefully handed over the bottle and regretfully heard the spirits departing. 'Thanks,' he said and was soon in close harmony with Oxy. Ghosts wouldn't wake him up. I listened to them for a while, and then joined in the chorus.

In the morning, I was the first one awake and was pleased to see clear sky through the cave mouth. There was plenty of dry firewood left from the previous night, and I was just arranging some kindling when it suddenly burst into flame.

I jumped back in surprise as a deep laughing voice said, 'Neat trick, that,' and he came into view sitting cross-legged beside me.

I said, 'Can't you knock or something – I don't want to start on the scotch this early.'

Len sat up and said, 'You're not still talking to yourself, you'll make me think this hole in the hill is haunted.' He took out his cigarettes, stuck one in his mouth; 'Thanks mate,' as it lit. He took it out of his mouth and sat looking at it, decided that if he said anything, he'd sound stupid, so he continued to smoke in silence, looking stupid instead.

Peters wasn't to be seen, but a long low whistle from the direction of Oxy's ear gave evidence of his whereabouts.

Oxy sat up, rubbing his eyes and said, 'Good morning, gentlemen. A fine day and all in good spirits, I trust.'

I must have been the only one to hear the soft chuckle that came from my seemingly vacant sleeping bag. 'These certainly beat miner's blankets.'

'Oh, shut up and get breakfast,' growled Len.

After breakfast, I went back to the cave where Peters had left his remains and I had no difficulty in locating the two spearheads. It was then that I began to realise that the gift of seeing and believing, given to me by the late prospector, was going to have its problems. As I stood up, with the spearheads in my hand, my flashlight illuminated the figures of two tall Aborigines, standing on either side of the late Mr Peters, in the most friendly manner imaginable. They were, no doubt, the two nightwatchmen responsible for the passing of Peters. As they spoke to each other in their ancient native tongue, I could see they were identifying the remains of their hunting spears, each one pointing to his own spearhead and indicating the position it had occupied in the body of their unfortunate victim.

Len suggested that I should not hang around the cave all day, so I raised my hand in friendly salute to the warriors, said it had been nice meeting the ex-prospector and was on my way with the spearheads, as well as some coins that had been lying in the dust, about where a pocket would have been.

Peters was awfully nice about it all, and said, 'Have a drink on me old chap – spirits of course.'

I showed my treasure to my companions who at first wanted to go back and see if they could find any more, but I said we had a long way to go and there was nothing else there.

We were about two hundred yards from the cave when I glanced back, and there in the entrance stood the tall, bearded Peters. Without thinking I raised my hand in farewell. Oxy was ahead of me and saw nothing, but Len saw my gesture and gave me quite a queer look. Then, glancing back, said, 'I'm sure I put the fire out, but it's still burning.'

'You must be seeing things, Len. Do you feel okay?'

'After the way you've been behaving ever since we got to the cave it wouldn't be any wonder if I didn't,' said Len. 'You've got me imagining things about the place with your yelling and talking to yourself – do you think it's haunted or something?'

Oxy heard the remark and said 'Don't tell me you believe in ghosts, Warner.'

'Aw, I don't know. There could be something in it.' said Len. 'What do you reckon?' turning to me as he spoke.

'Fair go, mate. You can't be serious.'

Then I changed the subject and started talking about the best track to the ridge we wanted to reach before dark. Just then a faint 'cooee' reached us from the direction of the cave, but I looked determinedly straight ahead and pretended I didn't hear it.

'Did you hear anything?' asked Len.

'Yeah, probably a plover or cockatoo or something,' said Oxy.

I said nothing. They wouldn't believe me anyway.

The trouble has been that, once I knew about ghosts, I've been seeing them in all sorts of unexpected places. All this nonsense about chains and things like that have no substance at all. They just couldn't support them. There is really nothing to be frightened about once you get to know them, and I quite often ignore them completely and walk straight through them.

One has to be careful, because you need to be quite sure it is a ghost. I've had some nasty collisions. They are a friendly crowd, and usually prefer to be left alone in their own particular haunts.

I was having a beer with Len and Oxy the other week and suggested another trip to the Bogongs. Oxy said something about being a bit overweight for hill climbing and thought he might go on a sea cruise next holidays. Len reckoned he'd like a bit of bird watching on the Gold Coast.

They had looked at each other a bit queer and neither suggested that I accompany them, so I said I might drive over to Perth and give the GTX a good tryout across the Nullarbor.

I was moving along nicely, and reckoned I could do the ton easily, when this tall, lean desert tribesman stepped across my port bow. Swerving like that was a purely reflex action, and proved fatal at that speed.

Of course, I should have just driven straight through him, but he showed up so suddenly.

I was pleased to see both Len and Oxy as pall bearers and I'm sure they were genuinely sorry. Fortunately, I didn't leave anyone else grieving.

As they walked out through the gates I couldn't resist it.

'So long, Oxy,' I said, and then, 'So long, Len.'

They looked at each other in some surprise and both said at once, 'Why did you say that?' Then the practical Oxy suggested that a beer wouldn't go astray, and off they went to down a couple. I looked on with the ghost of a smile and joined them in spirit.

Our Sergeant Major

I nearly wasn't going to include this story. I remember thinking that, when I first read it, several years ago, it seemed pretty weak in terms of plot. But, I decided to read it again, and have realised just how prescient Dad was. Remember that this was written in the 1970s. Not a lot has changed, in spite of all the changes that have happened.

No one in the football world was all that surprised when the morning papers announced in blazing banners that the Sergeant-Major had signed on for another three seasons.

In two seasons, he had brought a despondent team of wooden spooners into a grand final, and his reward for this effort had been gems of wisdom from the sports writers, with their twenty-twenty hindsight, telling their readers where and how he had failed.

They explained to the football-sated public just how the ten point defeat could have been converted to a ten goal victory, and how the writer, very early in the season, had pointed out his tactical weaknesses, and how the writer had reported the lack of confidence his team had in him.

All this after he had welded a group of individualists and raw recruits into a team that went into action as one man, a team whose small men had taken a season of hard knocks from the strong-arm, quick-elbow men of former top teams, who didn't take kindly to this incredibly fast element of the Sergeant-Major's company.

When he had come to coach the Eagles, Keith Sarjent was virtually unknown in the self-styled capital city of football. When research brought to light the fact that he had played only one season of league games in the West, big league in the East felt that their football prestige had been grossly insulted, especially since he was taking the place of the two-hundred-plus game bigshot with two Mighty Medals for best and fairest.

The sports brains of the press quickly forgot the lacing they had given the former coach at the end of his last season, because he had only twenty wins to his credit in four years of coaching.

One fast talking, slow thinking ex-star, now TV commentator, whose adoring followers had, unfortunately, given him the idea that he was something of a comedian, had, with the aid of a couple of budding script writers, referred to Keith as the Sergeant-Major of Company-E. The title stuck because it was an unwritten rule of footy protocol that coaches, players, and hangers-on must have nicknames, and no one else could be bothered thinking up a better one.

In appearance and approach, Keith was as unlike the popular image of an S.M. as you could find, but no one was ever long in his company before they became aware of his great love and knowledge of the game. No screaming fanatic, our Sergeant-Major, but he had a strength of character and quiet charm, plus an air of no-nonsense honesty that gave his Eagles a feeling of contagious confidence. The press had forgotten that his own playing career had ended in a car crash that had given him a permanently stiff elbow.

His ability to speak English in a well-modulated voice and effortless manner, without cliches, jargon, or football 'slanguage', left the popular commentator with inferiority complexes and frustrations that could only be soothed by the use of snide remarks as soon as he was off camera.

There was no doubting the brilliance of his football brain, and it was his gift of making his men listen and understand that was the foundation of his success. Don't get the idea that he wasn't a hard taskmaster. He knew the exact amount of physical training that each man needed, and though he never gave the impression of fanaticism himself, the team that ran out onto the field on Saturday was ready to devour lions, Christians, and gladiators alike for the honour and glory of Eagle Company.

He had an old fashioned idea that a team captain was chosen as a leader, not as a reward for having played more games than anyone else. On the ground, the captain was boss, and for a couple of hours, was infinitely more important than a coach. It was the captain's job to lead his men to victory, and unless Number One could get the support of the entire team, he wasn't worthy of the position.

That's where the sports writers came in.

'Who is the coach of Eagle Company, the captain or the Sergeant-Major?' Then they would wisely point out how captain Billy Bracken had, through his own leadership and brilliance, led his team of Davids to victory over the mighty Goliaths, and would finish their report with a question regarding the necessity or wisdom of buying an unknown into the team as a nominal coach.

Billy, and the rest of the team, would get hot under the collar and rise up in defence of Keith, who would laugh and say, 'Well we won again, that's the thing that counts. I just hope the other teams don't wake up to the fact that a good captain can make a good team into a premiership team.'

In short order, the once wooden spooners were stirring their rivals, and were only out of the final four on percentages in the first year, and within ten points of the flag at the end of the S.M.'s second season.

The big money, multi-premiership teams were worried. If rover Carlson of the Eagles hadn't been stretchered off early in the third quarter, the result could easily have gone the other way, and most likely would have. Ruckman Jarvis of the Devils was reported, and someone high up shook an admonishing finger at him and told him not to do it again. Keith congratulated the Devil's coach, looked him in the eye and said, 'I hadn't counted on your tactical brilliance in the third, I just never had a counter-move for it.'

Detective Inspector Jack Rowlands of the C.I.B., former captain of the Eagles, had retained his interest in the game, and the club, after his retirement from the game. He was now club president, and it was he who had first shown an interest in Keith Sarjent's coaching ability in the West. Jack had reason to visit the West to interview a business client who had considered that he would like to travel, but with other people's money. The detective had taken the opportunity to call on Keith while there.

By killing two birds with the one stone, Rowlands had returned with one bird secured by handcuffs, and the other by a contract for Sarjent to coach the Eagles for three years.

A firm friendship was formed between club president and coach, who soon became a frequent visitor to the Rowland's suburban home, and was a favourite with the whole family.

The Sergeant-Major held a position as accountant with a well-known and reputable finance company, whose managing director was also a committee member of the Eagles club. It was well known that, when living in the West, he had been in the employ of the same finance company, so that the transfer to the head office held no significance and was taken as a matter of course.

This, of course, was part of the coaching deal, and Keith knew that, time-wise, the job would not be too demanding, especially during the football season. Nevertheless, it was his policy that his fellow workers would have no reason to look upon him as a passenger. At the office, he was simply one of the team, and through his ability and urbanity, he was well-liked by his associates, more so when it became obvious that he was not going to look for promotions ahead of others who had been there before him.

In short, the golden boy of the Eagles was quite the perfect model of a modern Sergeant-Major. There wasn't anything in his past that his critics had been able to find to his detriment, and they tried hard enough. They were jolted back on their heels when one of them carried out some research on Westover Medal counting the season he had been rover for his former club. The umpires had been quite impressed with his dashing, speedy and fair play. There was no doubt about it, he kept all the Commandments, even to 'Thou shalt not be found out.'

The photographers and reporters, who snapped pictures and penned items for the 'What People Did at the Weekend' pages in the glossy magazines, followed him in droves. The result was an endless stream of articles about the football world's most charming, most handsome and most eligible, as he partnered the preened and polished parade of birds of paradise in their finest feathers, to all the nicest social functions. Despite the glittering ground-bait scattered across the surface of the social pool, it failed to make Keith rise to take the hook, and he still remained popular, sought after, and unattached.

His phone number was not listed; he lived on an 'I'll ring you' agreement with all and sundry, except for his closest friends. It was known that he had a comfortable, serviced flat in the heart of Eagle territory. Nobody seemed to know anybody who had been invited to his home, though it could be safely assumed that people such as

Rowlands, Bracken and so on, were welcome visitors there. At least they never said they were not.

During interviews by TV or press journalists, if asked about what he did in his spare time, he would mention films, dancing and squash, so that they were always left with the feeling that he didn't have any private life at all. Various generous figures had been mentioned regarding the remuneration he received for his services, and when questioned about the battered antiquity of his car, he'd laugh in genuine amusement and say, 'Oh, I wouldn't part with that, it's all the family I have, and I really only need it to get me to the ground if I'm running late.' After another chuckle, he'd be likely to add something to the effect that, even then, it would be quicker to simply keep on running.

His closest and most constant friendship was with the Rowlands family, and he was often a weekend visitor to their very comfortable home during the off-season. The fact that Jack Rowlands was one of the finest top men in the police force didn't stop people from wondering how he could afford to live in such luxury. His was one of the best homes in the area.

Certain sections of the public are always ready, willing and able to cast aspersions at members of the force if they acquire anything beyond the reach of the casters, but if Jack was ever aware of it, he apparently didn't let it worry him.

Sarjent must have been content with life, because he never paid any visits to friends or relatives back in the West. Except for an occasional fishing safari with Jack, he was satisfied to stay put, to enjoy his social outings.

The approach of his third season as coach found him as keen and as popular as ever, and the luck of the draw brought the two grand finalists of last year together early in the season.

The sports writers wrote many pages of wise predictions about the outcome of the game, which would prove beyond doubt the superiority of the Devils. Rumour had it that Bracken told the Devils' ruckman that if Carlson was injured in any way during the game, then he could consider himself somewhat accident prone, and may not even see the season out. This, of course, was emphatically denied at one of the numerous post-mortems of the match.

It was quite noticeable, however, that the dashing rover spearheaded the now famous flying squad of Eagle Company. Time and time again, their brilliance left their bigger opponents bothered and bewildered, as the ball travelled rapidly in the direction of goal. The small men played the ball, and the big men played guardians to them to such effect that the mighty were humbled. Once again, the S.M. was unperturbed when the critics, in their wisdom, gave Bracken and Carlson all the credit for the fine win. He was also lavish in his praise of them.

Towards the end of the season, it appeared that the grand final would again be between the 'Two deadliest rivals in the history of our great National Game', with no apologies to flannelled fools, the sport of kings, or the northern states. The Saturday before the grand final 'Our Sport Spy' in the morning press reported that:

'... coach Keith Sarjent would be relaxing at the home of his friend D.I. Jack Rowlands, while Captain Morgan's Pirates and the Devils decided which team earned the right to face up to the Sergeant Major's Company E. on the big parade ground next week.'

That night, after the final replay of the game, the two friends sat relaxed in the centrally-heated, and well-padded comfort of the Rowland's lounge room.

'It's been a good season, Keith. Win or lose against the Devils next week, the job is yours for another three seasons, if you want it'

'On whose terms, Rowlands?' The adoring public would have been shocked at the hardness of the voice and the lack of friendship in the direct, blue eyes.

'As far as I'm concerned, the same terms,' said the detective.

The coach took a sip of scotch, and it seemed as though he had lost the thread of the conversation when he remarked, 'Quite a cosy pad here, for a cop. Does anyone ever ask you how you did it?' That surely wasn't the golden boy speaking.

The reply was not at all friendly, 'You've enjoyed the comforts often enough.'

At that moment, the door opened and Janet Rowlands entered the room. She was tall, slim and attractive and made no attempt at hiding the little bit of grey beginning to silver her dark hair. She turned off the television and said, 'Are you two going to sit here all night talking football?'

Both men laughed, and once again the public would have recognised the S.M.

'Just having a nightcap dear. You go along, you know how jumpy Keith gets when the pressure is on.'

She looked down at the relaxed, smiling coach, said good night and left them.

'I can't get used to a big, tough cop being in love,' the quiet voice was sarcastic. 'How much do you want to win next Saturday, Mr President?'

'If we lose next week, you'll know how much I wanted the flag.'

The coach was still relaxed, cool, but his eyes were hard. Then suddenly the mouth smiled as he said, almost in a whisper, 'How would you like me for a son-in-law?'

In one lithe movement the detective was on his feet and grabbing the coach's jacket, jerking him to his feet.

The Sergeant Major's expression never altered, 'Don't wake the family, Dad.'

The detective was angry. 'If you lay a finger on Jenny, I'll break your back.'

'Oh, don't be so early-Victorian, Inspector. You didn't seem to mind when the popular coach was seen dancing with the attractive elder daughter of his best friend at the 'Quiet Knight' club last week.'

Somehow, he still managed to look unflappable, and the angry man released him. The coach resumed his comfortable position, held his glass to the light, 'Glenfiddich, and you almost made me spill it,' and took another appreciative sip. The big man stood looking down at him, trying to keep his temper.

'I only have to crook my finger at Jenny and she'd come running, you know that. She'll be twenty this year, won't she? Fourteen years isn't much of a difference. Did I ask you how much you want the flag?'

'You are a hypocrite, a swindler and a thief and I could have you locked up for ten years.'

'And you, Detective Inspector, would sell your brat of a girl for a game of football – you and I both know that. Okay, there's a bit more involved, like your good name, your comfortable home, your police pension, your wife, and maybe a few years of freedom. We might spend ten years locked up together, and you'd still be young enough to enjoy life, providing you never met any of your old friends.' The coach tossed down the rest of his drink, rose slowly to his feet and placed a gentle hand on the big man's chest. The big man stepped back. Sarjent smiled as he said, 'I'm off to bed, the bridegroom needs his beauty sleep.'

Again, the detective's hands gripped the smaller man's jacket. With the same benign smile, Sarjent said, 'Three stone lighter and only one good arm, what would the family say?'

'Sit down, you and I are going to settle this right now.' The coach was sat down suddenly and firmly in the chair he had just left. He calmly poured himself another drink and relaxed again.

The detective thrust his hands into his pockets. He looked tired, he felt old. 'You know, if you step one inch out of line, the C.I.B. in the West will get a package of information that will put you inside.' He walked across the room, came back and sat down. When he spoke again, it was the voice of a man with the situation well in hand. 'In fact, I'll go further than that, Sarjent,' he swivelled his chair so that he faced the reclining figure, 'if we don't win the flag next week, I'll see that they get the evidence.'

He got to his feet and was about to leave the room when the soft voice of Sarjent said, 'Oh, Inspector. Please forgive me for never having invited you to my flat before this. Tomorrow, when you drive me home, you must come up and hear some of my tapes. I'm quite an enthusiast you know. Did you know that some of them were taken in this very room? You're a fool Rowlands, you know my background yet you were too conceited to think I could get anything on you. The room's bugged, it's a hobby; you can go searching for them tomorrow – don't forget to check under your chair. It's amazing the advances that have been made in electronic and wireless surveillance. Everything you've said since the TV was turned off is on tape in my room. I'll give it to you for a souvenir. I've got plenty of others that will come to light if something happens to me.'

The detective was silent, there didn't seem to be anything for him to say. Then the coach's mocking voice went on, 'Incidentally, Jenny and I are going to the Beethoven recital tomorrow night. She loves music,' he paused, 'and good company.'

Anger flared again in the policeman's eyes, 'Okay, Sarjent, you're off the hook, as long as you leave Jenny alone.' Anger was in his voice.

'Any back pay, Inspector? You don't know how I've missed all those lovely cheques from the Eagles Club that never got past the president.'

'No, damn you. You've bought your freedom and you're in the clear. Not only that, you can name your price as coach, the Devils have already approached me.'

'Yes, I can, thanks to Captain Bracken who knows more about football than any two-bit coach from the West.' He shook his head in mock sorrow. 'You and I could have been a good team, Inspector.'

Then, suddenly, the well-known smile appeared, 'Don't you think I want the flag as much as you do? I've never done anything crooked in football, and never will. Those boys trust me, Rowlands. I'll sign on again if you and the team want me, but I had to get myself off the hook – you know that.' He rose and was leaving the room when he turned with his hand on the door handle. There was no trace of a smile as he said, 'Don't go looking for tapes, Jack, I need the insurance. Good night.'

The following afternoon the Sergeant Major made a guest appearance on Sport World, and when asked about his future in football, he said, 'Jack Rowlands asked if I wanted to renew my contract, and there is a fair chance that I will. That's all I'll say on the matter right now.' Then the beatific smile appeared as he added, 'Two flags would be nice.'

So, no one in the football world was all that surprised when the morning papers announced that the Sergeant Major had signed on for another three years – win or lose next Saturday.

Gone Bush

S TEVE WAS ALWAYS THE one who came up with the bright ideas. 'Look, Mack,' he said to me one day, 'what's the point in hanging around home all the holidays doing nothing. Dad and Mum will be working, and it's just going to be great washing breakfast dishes, getting our own lunch and doing the housework. Then Mum'll say, you can get tea started, seeing as you've nothing else to do. Let's go bush.'

'Bush?' I said, and made it sound like a question. 'Shall we leave a forwarding address so the Rescue Squad can find us and lead us home? If you walked across the park, you'd have to ask which way to get back – you've got to know what you're doing when you go bush.'

Steve considered the wisdom of my statement for a few seconds. 'Yeah, and we'll find out all we need to know sitting here all the week in front of TV and arguing. You only have to use a bit of common sense and know where you're going and about how long it will take.

'This is what we could do – a one-way ticket each to Coonabah, twenty dollars each, at the most, and the bus goes up there Mondays – here look at the map – head south from Coonabah to Mitchell, do it by Friday evening, and Dad and Mum could come up and pick us up there on Saturday.'

I had to admit that it did sound inviting, and expenses wouldn't be any higher than if we stayed home eating biscuits and fruit all day. Steve could always talk me into anything. He was big and dark and pretty solid.

Dad and Mum had given me a two-man tent for my birthday, and I'd been intending to use it at Christmas. You could get some pretty wild conditions in the hills in September, but as Steve said, 'They're hardly what you'd call mountains, and winter is practically over by then – look it's only a stone's throw from Coonabah to Mitchell.'

In fact, it was only two or three inches on the map, so I said we'd see what Dad said when he got home. Then we could find out if Jimmy Grant was interested. Then we'd talk about it some more. I was a more cautious type than Steve and I knew he wasn't very impressed with my suggestions, but it was more acceptable to him than a straight out 'no'.

I had turned sixteen two months ago. Steve and Jimmy were both one class behind me.

We had just got in from school and Steve had been studying the road map ever since we had come into our room. Karen's bag was on the kitchen table, so we guessed that she was at Julie's place. I stretched out on my bed – a day's school can be wearying, you know – thinking I'd better get out of my school uniform and hang it up before Mum came in. Steve was having one of his spells of being an exemplary younger son and was in jeans and pullover, his uniform already hanging in the wardrobe. I should have known he had something in mind.

I turned my head and looked at him absorbed in the map and his holiday plans. He'd even had his hair cut recently and had brushed it since he'd come in – boy, he was really keen on this hike.

'Have you cleaned your shoes?'

'Yeah, when I came in. Why?' then he gave me that grin that could make Julie's older sister go weak at the knees, and said, 'Well, if you want something, you gotta work at it.'

'Like English?' Mum was always onto us about that, and in case he got the idea I was a passenger in the team, I changed into some cords (Steve's in fact) and dragged on the wind cheater Dad had been looking for last night. Then I hung up my uniform and put my shoes away – they didn't need polishing.

I put Karen's bag on a kitchen chair – 'Why can't you put your things away like the boys do?' another point for the boys – looked in the fridge and saw a casserole ready for the oven.

I never could remember if I should turn the oven on first or put the casserole in and then turn it on. Then I set the table.

There was an epidemic of giggles at the back door and Karen came in, followed by Julie and Christine Barrett. Steve heard them and came out to practice his grin. Not that he cared two hoots for girls, it just amused him to see Chris go ga-ga when she saw him. I wondered what it was like to have that sort of effect on girls.

Chris was okay, if only she kept out of sight of little brother – who was not so little and was already handing his clothes down to me, but I could still leave him in my dust over any distance from 100 yards to a mile. Steve was going on with his endless patter and I thought I'd soon have to help Chris to a chair. Then he said, 'Students must study, children,' and went back to his room. Chris gave a soul shattering sigh and said, 'Hi, Mack,' as if she'd just come in. I wished I had Steve's grin.

'You running next week?' she asked.

'Yeah, the one hundred, two hundred and the four-by-four.'

'Gee, you're good,' and I felt as though I'd evened Steve for once. There was actually some admiration in her eyes. I knew I'd kill them in the sprints and could make up fifty yards in the relay if I had to. Just then Mum came in and said, right on cue, 'Karen, why can't you put – oh, hello, Chris.'

'Hi, Mrs Macklin, come on Julie, Mum'll be looking for us.'

Dad was reading *The Herald* when Steve said, 'Hey Dad, can we go hiking next week?'

'Hmm, I guess so,' from Dad without looking up. Steve poked me with his toe.

'Thought we'd fly up to Broome and walk across, through Mt Isa, and you could pick us up at Cairns if you're not doing anything on the weekend.'

'Golf Saturday morning, that's all,' and went back to his reading.

So Steve said, 'Have a good day at the office, Jim?'

'Pretty normal, dear.'

Mum pretended to look annoyed, but giggled and said, 'Behave yourself, Stephen.'

'Yes, Dear,' said Stephen.

Dad looked up and realised what was going on. I suppose there was a time when Mum used to swoon about the grin that Steve had inherited. Mum still had the sprinter's figure, though.

'Go hiking, did you say. Anywhere in particular?'

Steve outlined his project and Dad said he'd think about it. Which meant he and Mum would talk about it without our help and she would tell him what he thought about it.

It was nearly one o'clock when Steve, Jimmy and I left the bus at Coonabah on the Monday, so we decided to have a pie and a drink at the Milk Bar, and get moving straight away.

Jimmy's uncle had got hold of some maps from the Forestry Commission. They had quite a lot of detail about four-wheel drive tracks and creeks that never showed up on road maps, as well as a lot of information on the topography of the area. So, all we had to do was keep on a course due south and we'd hit the river, which we could follow to Mitchell. Even an error of several miles wouldn't make that much difference. We'd kill the distance in five full days and what was left of today.

We had gone over the maps a dozen times and had divided it up into sections so that we would have a creek to camp beside every night. We were quite confident that they would all be running at this time of year, so one bottle of water each was all we'd need to carry.

We'd scrounged around among our mates in forms four and five and borrowed rucksacks and all the other gear we were short of from schoolmates, most of whom reckoned they were too intelligent to want them at that time of the year.

From Coonabah, the access road was good, and we knocked off the fifteen miles to our first scheduled stop without raising a sweat or a blister. It was a beautiful Spring day, conditions just could not have been better, even our camp site was ideal with a crystal clear, ice-cold creek and a springy mat of gum leaves.

I'd have preferred to stay there for the whole week and even suggested it to Steve, but that didn't suit his more adventurous spirit. Funny how people are different. I was the sprinter and worked hard at keeping in top condition, but could relax anywhere, any time and dream the hours away.

Physically, Steve was the plodding type, but with an amazing capacity to study, yet at the same time to think constructively for himself and he always wanted to be somewhere else, to keep on moving.

Jimmy was a quiet, easy going character, popular with everyone and could yarn away with kids or oldies with complete unconcern on so many subjects that he should have got A pluses in everything instead of only most subjects. When we asked him how he did it he'd say, 'Aw, I don't know. When I read something, I remember it, that's all. If I had to work it out for myself, I'd be lost. Too lazy, I guess.' He was a fount of information on the history of the area we were crossing. 'There was a book about it in the library, so I thought it would be good to know who had been here, and when. There was a bit of alluvial gold through most of it, but no big finds, and most of it too steep and rocky for agriculture. That's why it's nearly all Forestry Commission land.'

The second day, after we had crossed the creek, we began to learn something about the rugged nature of the terrain, but we still had a track to follow, one suitable for four-wheel-drive fire fighting units. Somewhat up and down, but mostly up.

The spot we had marked for a camp site that night was the end of the track, marked on the map with an asterisk, which the legend told us, 'No vehicles beyond this point'. It had been another fine day with still an hour's daylight left, but there were clouds banking up from the south, and the wind was cold. We had expected cold, wet weather and were prepared for it. We got it.

By midnight, it was pelting down. We only had the one tent, so had decided that, in the event of heavy rain at night, we'd just have to play at being the three wise monkeys and sit in a row in the tent. The three little porcelain monkeys that sat in a row on Karen's bookshelf never looked as tired and sorry as we must have looked, but we weathered it pretty well, in our sleeping bags with knees up under our chins. No rain came in, so we were dry and warm. We didn't sleep though. The wind shrieked through the tops of the trees and we wondered if any of them would come down on top of us, or if any would be left standing at all.

Pitch black night, pouring rain, and if you haven't slept out in it, you can't believe the amount of noise the wind can make in tall timber. We could only sit and pretend we were not scared stiff. The only good thing about it was that we couldn't see how scared we looked.

There was too much noise to carry on a conversation, and a couple of times we even made some attempt to sing, but we were not songbirds. I wondered how the birds were faring and reckoned we were better off than they were. Every few minutes, Steve looked at his watch, but that didn't help things at all. A dozen times he said it was stopped and flicked on the flashlight to see if the second hand was still moving.

By five o'clock the gale had dropped, but the rain was still heavy, and when watery daylight showed through the tent walls, Jimmy slid the zip open a few inches to have a look out and said, 'Pity we didn't cross the creek last night, it's not there now.'

'What do you mean, it's not there?' asked Steve.

'There's a river there now.'

By sunrise, the rain had stopped, and apart from a scattering of fresh twigs and leaves, everything looked the same as last night. Everything, that is, except the creek.

We had a midget gas stove – just a little burner on top of a can – to use in case of a lack of dry wood.

'We won't need much coffee in the cups this morning – the water already looks like coffee,' remarked Steve.

On Dad's advice we had brought oatmeal and powdered milk. 'Light to carry and just add water – nothing like it on a cold morning.' He was eating eggs on toast and drinking orange juice as he said it.

That morning we could have eaten a gallon of porridge each. During breakfast we discussed the best tactics on how to cross the creek and stay dry, but finally decided we were all going to take a very cold plunge.

The length of nylon cord was more than enough to reach across, and as Jimmy was the best swimmer, we elected him to go first – two votes to one. The water was running fast, but not dangerously so. He went in fast and came out the other side faster, and a delicate shade of blue – that water was cold.

He tied his end of the rope to a tree, low down and we pulled it tight, high up on our side, while he stamped around shivering and yelling at us to hurry up. Then we sent his bundle of clothing, and a towel, sliding down the rope. He broke all records drying and dressing. Then we sent the rest of our gear over in the same manner and it was our turn to do a freeze.

It was good to get started up the hill on the south side of the creek and get some warmth into our bones.

By mid-morning we were in high spirits again and making good time, despite the uphill climb through the undergrowth.

I've always had a "thing" about the bush. That morning, in the cold bracing air, with the sky clearing of cloud and no visible threat of further rain, was when I knew that I'd have to spend all the time I possibly could studying the Australian bush and making a career for myself, somehow or other, in an organisation designed to protect and preserve our flora and fauna. Steve never knew how much his harebrained idea of a bush walk meant to me now.

According to our map, we were on the highest point of the hike. It was lunchtime, and it seemed as though we could see for a hundred miles in every direction. Away to the north-east there were snowy tops. To the south, the hills lessened in ruggedness suggesting that the rest of the trip would be easy and leisurely – not exactly like walking down Collins Street, mind you, but no trouble to young men with more energy than brains.

'Come on, dreamer, we've got a few miles to go to the next creek and I want an early tea and ten hours sleep.' Steve woke me out of my reverie and we were on our way. Steve and Jimmy kept up the conversation while I hung back a bit to enjoy the surroundings.

That night, we all slept from dark to daylight and woke to another calm, clear morning. The whole world seemed to sparkle. All that morning, we had bellbirds for company with cheerful willie wagtails fluttering ahead of us and darting almost into our faces. Occasionally, the scarlet flash of a king parrot would show between the branches, and time and time again, kookaburras saw the humour of the situation. The wattle was practically finished, except in deep, shaded valleys here and there, where they bloomed later and held their blossom longer. There were splashes of purple native mint already in bloom, and in places we could walk knee-deep in heath from palest pink to crimson.

I was determined that by this time next year there would not be a plant or flower or bird along this track that I couldn't name – the bush had got to me.

Steve and Jimmy were continually calling me to hurry up. 'Pack getting too heavy, Sonny? I'll carry it for you if you like.' The things you have to put up with from kid brothers. As he turned to say it he tripped on a branch and executed an unscheduled forward roll. 'Come on, Sonny, we can have a rest at lunchtime. I told you this wasn't a picnic for kids.'

The next two days were easy enough, and the weather was good. We could hear the movement of possums in the trees around us at night and a pair of boo-book owls insulted each other from one hilltop to the next.

By Friday evening, we were in the foothills and in view of Mitchell when it clouded over and drizzled a couple of times during the night. It was my turn to sleep out. My ground sheet kept me dry from below while a light plastic cover kept the rain off. It wasn't cold in the sleeping bag, in fact I enjoyed the light rain and the smell of the damp leaves and earth too much to disturb the others who didn't even know it had been raining until morning.

We reached the town late on Friday morning and took possession of the motel unit that Dad had booked for us. By the time the family station wagon came into view, we had showered and dined – pies and coke. Once again, we were sitting in a row like the three wise monkeys but feeling more comfortable than we had felt when sitting in the tent listening to the wind.

We stayed overnight at the motel, and I had to admit that beds are good to sleep in. We told Karen all sorts of wild yarns about the dangers we had overcome, but kid sisters are not easily impressed.

Sunday afternoon, Julie and Chris called in to see Karen.

Steve turned on his million-dollar smile. Chris said, 'Hi, Steve,' like he was a kid brother, and turned a dazzling, blue-eyed look of adulation on me and said, 'Can I see your three gold medals, Mack? Gee, you were great.'

Steve shoved a chair against the back of my knees. 'Okay, Champ, I can't win them all.'

Winding Back

―――◆―――

This is an autobiographical story that happened, I think, in the early 1980s. Dad travelled to Port Broughton, his birthplace, with his best friend, and then on to Ward's Hill (the apostrophe has since been officially removed). Dad's father had a wheat farm at Ward's Hill.

JUST DON'T BELIEVE IT when anyone tells you that nostalgia isn't what it used to be. I was only a bit of a kid, hadn't even started school, when Dad sold the wheat farm at Warden and we moved to a dairy farm, and then it was nearly fifty years before I made the effort to get back and find out what the farm and the country around about were really like. The recollections I had were vague and mainly remembered because of the many-times told tales of parents and friends.

I was surprised and delighted, completely enchanted, by the charm and beauty of the pastel-tinted wheat fields with their backdrop of low, mist-blue hills, covered here and there with the deep purple of Patterson's curse; no doubt a beautiful affliction with which to be cursed.

What a glorious drive in late spring sunshine through the rolling, folding, ever changing kaleidoscope. You could feel the quiet contentment of the peaceful countryside and the beauty of the little bustling country town, named many years ago by some Irishman, homesick for the county of soft greenness that he'd left thousands of weary miles behind.

Our eyes caught, and our minds beheld, the loveliness of the little town nestling in its sheltering hills. It would seem that the town itself was in love with the contrasting surroundings. Gum tree-clad hills, vineyards and wheat fields, all seemed to be within arm's-reach of the busy little heart of it.

It was pleasant enough to steal a couple of days off when I should have been getting into top gear for the normal end of the year rush. To be able to persuade a close friend into doing the same made it doubly pleasant. Then, just to double up again, the added gift of glorious weather and lovely, unfamiliar surroundings, was enough to turn two staid fathers of adult families into a pair of footloose freebooters.

So what if two thirds or more of our allotted spans had passed us by, and what if our buckle was more in evidence than our swash. We were as happy as hippies and we sang as we drove, and laughed together at every damn silly thing we said to each other, even if it wasn't funny.

We pulled into a roadhouse for lunch, and as we loitered over a cup of coffee, asked each other which direction we'd head next and came to no definite conclusion. In fact, neither of us cared much if we just put our heels up right there where we were for the rest of the weekend.

The driver of a car with caravan attached nodded in greeting as we walked out and then said, 'What's the road like from here to Warden?' We said we didn't know, we were also Victorians, and I said to my companion in crime, 'If he can go to Warden, so can we, after all, it has some claim to fame. I was born there.'

So, instead of heading north to unveil the magic mysteries of the blue-hazed ranges, we cut a track across the beginnings of them.

At least I know now that the road from there to Warden is smooth and easy travelling, though a large part of it is unsealed and dusty. There were very few cars on it to make the dust fly, and we had no difficulty in keeping ahead of our own. It is a typical Australian country scene, that of a car moving easily and quickly past the browning wheat fields and the purpling hills, towing behind it its own personal trailer of dust. Even the colour of the dust varies from time to time depending on the topping used in the road surfacing. Sometimes, as the breeze strengthened, it would disperse almost immediately, while at others, it just stayed put in the still, warm air.

Nostalgia really set in when we finally reached the township, and memories stored away in little secret places came bustling back, like ghosts of dead times, places and people.

The pub was still there, thank goodness, circa 1910. Square, solid, two stories, and it should still be there in another fifty years or more.

It's good to get back among buildings that are constructed in the old style from the local limestone or sandstone. They seem to be part of the landscape.

The beer was cool, and the dust of travel quickly vanished from our throats. There was only a dozen or so in the bar. They had been there too long, even at that early hour, so we debated the subject of our neighbours' characters, and decided we were no longer thirsty.

For us, it was down with the demon drink. For me, it was to drink deeply of years ago. That place across the street would have been the tearooms we'd visit whenever we came in from the farm in the buggy. Suddenly, the vision of the back ends of two horses filled the wide screen of memory. The busy little black pony, whose hooves twinkled as he spanked along, beside the tall leisurely bay.

I remember once the school teacher who boarded with us

borrowed the two-wheeled sulky and little black 'Ebony' one afternoon. She was caught in a sudden shower and was extremely wet and bedraggled on her return.

'Didn't you take an umbrella?' asked Dad.

'Yes,' she replied, 'but you did say to keep the rain off his tail.'

'No,' replied Dad, 'I said keep the reins off his tail.'

Oh yes, the tearooms, I had a crush on the proprietress, and if one slice of fruit cake happened to be bigger than the rest, I knew she had meant it for me.

Just along the street had been the hardware store, run by one of those wonderful old people who can only be described as a gentleman. A close friend of my parents, his byword was honesty. He lived to a great old age and kept in touch to the end of his days, many years after we'd gone from the district.

Honesty seemed to be taken for granted in the community there. They lived and worked in harmony and trust. These people were true neighbours to each other.

We took a stroll along the jetty. A good long one it is too, crossing an expanse of shallow water over oozy looking mud to the deep channel of what was once a busy little wheat port. The sailing clippers called there once. The wheat was brought from the farms on the big, broad-tyred wagons behind teams of eight or ten horses. Dad was proud of his team, and like many of his contemporaries, was a wonderful handler of draught horses. It took real teamwork to get a heavily laden wagon moving on sandy soil. He had the ability to get each horse leaning into its collar in perfect unison with the others.

The jetty had recently been renovated, and a costly job it would have been too, so some local industry must warrant the expense. The fishing was always good and the whiting of the finest quality, so it could perhaps be there in commercial quantity.

But, let's go looking for the old farm, maybe I'll know it when we get there. Maybe I'll even take the right road. There aren't many to choose from.

A quick visit to the World War One memorial. The old familiar figure, 'How sturdy and staunch he stands'. The list of names of those who enlisted from thereabouts was as loaded with memories of neighbours and friends of friends as if I'd known them myself, even the ones on the special honour roll who went with a good will and had not come back.

It must have been around the turn of the century, now three quarters of a century gone, when Dad moved onto the farm. The house looked just as I knew it should look. From every prominence was seen the glimmer of the gulf, not faded one iota in the passing years. There was only salty wasteland between the back fence, four miles from the front gate, and the sea.

The foundation stone on the sturdy little church nearby informed us that it had stood there for seventy years. The congregation had long since departed, and the building was out of use and out of repair. For many years it had also been used as a school, all my sisters attended there. For the older ones, it was the only school they had attended.

Another of Dad's good friends had the farm next door, and I have memories of a laconic sun-browned farmer, small of stature but large in neighbourliness. Two typical comments of his came immediately to mind. Commenting on his inconvenient lack of inches he remarked, 'Too much darned leg turned up for foot.' The other quote came about through assisting another neighbour to execute one of the more unpleasant tasks of country living.

The proverbial out-building was always constructed at a sensible distance from the house – 'stuck out' in fact. Usually a whacking great hole was dug and the edifice erected over it. With the passing of time the hole filled and something had to be done about it. This meant another hole was dug nearby, and either the building or the contents moved from one to the other, whichever was considered the quickest and easiest. In this particular case, they decided to move the contents per media of the good old kerosene-tin bucket and, as was thought proper, the owner toiled in the old hole while good neighbour attended to transportation and deposition.

He was terribly contrite when he allowed a bucketful to return to sender upside down and unexpectedly. Explanation and contrition were given together in a quiet sentence. 'The darned thing slipped.'

Cricket was, perhaps, one of the most popular pastimes in the off seasons between 'plough and harrow, plant and sow' and harvest time. Now, where the cricket ground once was, there is a couple of tennis courts, and a couple of dozen enthusiasts enjoying a lovely Saturday afternoon. I know I'd have been made welcome in the warm, friendly manner of country folk had I ventured in and said, 'This land is blessed by the memory of my father whose land it was.' But we contented ourselves in watching the scene from the 'road gate' and clicking a camera so that next week, on being woken to reality, we could prove it was not a dream at all.

People travel to distant lands – and why shouldn't they – at great expense. But, for a cornball like me, there was an inexpressible pleasure in the day's jaunt and I realise why my parents so often wound back their own memories to the old days in this wonderful wheat district. Their's was the pioneering spirit that knew hard work and the heartbreak that was part of life, love and contentment. The incidents that came most often to their minds were the ones that brought laughter in reliving the good times.

There was no time left for us to dally if we wanted to dine and sleep in comfort, so we did an about turn to the bit of Ireland that wasn't Irish. We placed the sun behind our left ears and travelled again over the dusty roads.

The sleepy lizards – the slow old bobtails – haven't moved with the times, and they take their lives in their hands, or whatever they've got, whenever they cross the road. I caught a couple, just to see if they remembered me, and put them in a place of greater safety. They are quite unobtrusive fellows completely lacking in malice, nor are they addicted to hypertension and the pressures of civilisation.

The lesson of the lizard, or the quiet surroundings, or maybe the fact that we are no longer callow youths made for a leisurely drive, but we were still in time for a beer, a motel room and a most enjoyable meal, after which we slept like the good kids we are.

The camera clicked again – to help us remember the view – from Billy Goat Hill. Persons of lesser character would have taken the opportunity, no doubt, of converting our weekend of freedom to a lost weekend, but they'd have enjoyed it less.

It's unlikely that my travelling companion will ever be forced to read these few words, but if by some strange chance he does, may I say, 'Thank you, Jim.'

www.ingramcontent.com/pod-product-compliance
Lightning Source LLC
Chambersburg PA
CBHW032037290426
44110CB00012B/841